JOE PETA'S TOUR
GUIDE PRESENTS:

A 2019 MASTERS
PREVIEW

JOE PETA

To Matt,

Who should be included in everyone's dream foursome

To Scott, Tim and Tom,

Who taught me long ago the depth of a friendship can be measured by the speed with which the same $20 bill changes hands after the weekly golf outing

Contents

JOE PETA'S TOUR GUIDE PRESENTS:

A 2019 MASTERS PREVIEW

JOE PETA

Introduction

In the midst of researching my 2017 Major League Baseball team outlook pieces on deadline for ESPN.com, I received an e-mail from a holycross.edu address. The writer, Matthew Croglio, informed me that he'd been a fan of my Wall Street, sabermetric, and baseball betting memoir, *Trading Bases*. Inspired by the book, he'd created a model to bet on PGA Tour events while he was in college. Further, he added, he'd been writing a weekly golf newsletter for his friends with suggested bets for that week's tournament and he thought maybe I'd like to see it.

The weekly letter distinguished itself as both entertaining and informative. Informative because it was packed with fascinating, granular course and player data I didn't know existed. One key term, Strokes Gained, did ring a bell. I wondered if these statistics were related to the work of a professor I had met a few years earlier when I was promoting *Trading Bases*.

Three years earlier, I had spoken at a Santa Fe Institute-organized event hosted by a large Wall Street bank. The other speakers included Michael Mauboussin, author of, among other books, *The Success Equation*; a Fidelity Investments Portfolio Manager who was an expert in hockey analytics; and a Columbia Professor named Mark Broadie, who told the audience about the Strokes Gained concept he'd developed working with PGA Tour data. I remembered his riveting talk about putting but didn't think too much more about it at the time. Truthfully, owing to the combination of my baseball work and the departure of an injured Tiger Woods from the sport's stage, I hadn't even watched much golf for a few years.

However, sparked by the weekly e-mail I received, I turned on that week's Genesis Open, and wouldn't you know it, some of the data had made its way onto the broadcast.

After the third round of the tournament, CBS golf announcer Amanda Balionis interviewed tournament leader Dustin Johnson. Despite having just carded a seven-under-par 64 on the famed Riviera Golf Course, DJ, as he's know to golf fans everywhere, mentioned he had areas of his game to work on. Balionis, standing in front of a large interactive video board she'd earlier used to display Strokes Gained statistics, asked him if he'd look at "the data" to help aid his work. Johnson smirked, looking as if he were about to answer smugly, and then thought better of it. He replied, in what sounded like a diplomatic tone, something to the effect of, "No, I'll figure it out with a club on the range."

Ben Hogan would have loved that answer. By all accounts a prickly individual, Hogan, one of only five golfers to complete the career Grand Slam, was said to consistently answer those who asked him to reveal the key to a good golf swing with a terse, "the secret is in the dirt." For a PGA Tour professional, it's almost certainly the case that practice and repetition on the range are how swings are mastered and refined. To succeed on the PGA Tour, nay, to even *get* to the PGA Tour, you need to spend a lifetime "in the dirt."

For the newest generation of analytics-driven golf fans, however, the secret to *enjoying* golf isn't in the dirt, it's in the data. Knowing how long it had taken baseball broadcasters to recognize the existence of its data-happy fans, at least without mocking them, I found it encouraging CBS had embraced this new approach to revealing performance on the golf course for its viewers.

I made a note to explore it further, but as my immersion into baseball writing, along with a full-time job in the financial industry, consumed all of my productive time, another year passed. Last winter though, I made the decision to take a sabbatical from baseball writing and dive as deeply as possible into the world of golf data. This preview of the 2019 Masters Tournament is the first product of that research.

Besides Professor Broadie's groundbreaking work, there's some great content created regularly for today's breed of golf fans. The guys at datagolf.ca, brothers Matt and Will Courchene, create tremendous data visualizations of PGA data and have created the template for what I believe every modern leaderboard should look like. I've learned more about golf course architecture than I thought possible from Andy Johnson and Will Knights of thefriedegg.com and @the_fried_egg. No one who is under the age of 40 should consider themselves a golf fan if they are unfamiliar with the rollicking podcasts and Twitter musings of the guys behind the No Laying Up website and Twitter account.

While they, among others, make golf fandom more enjoyable in the social media age, my familiarity with the four-decade history of baseball's sabermetric community suggests that the golf side of the equation is still ~~in the early innings~~ in its early stages, about the middle of the 4th fairway of a round of golf, if you will. If greater access to data and novel ways to assess performance increase your attachment to any sport, and if you prefer skill-based analysis over results-based narratives, my hope is this book will enhance your enjoyment of the greatest golf tournament in the world.

To rolling 'em smooth,

Joe
@MagicRatSF
MastersTourGuide@gmail.com

Chapter 1

Tiger Woods is Even Better than You Think, Part I

The late Bum Phillips, who spent four decades coaching high school, college and pro football, once said of Bear Bryant, the legendary head coach of Alabama, "Bryant can take his'n and beat your'n, and then he can turn around and take your'n and beat his'n." That's the ultimate compliment for a head coach because it flies in the face of conventional wisdom that the team with the better players will win. Or as Phillips, a native Texan known for both his omnipresent cowboy hat and his homespun wisdom might say, "it's not about the Jimmys and the Joes, it's about the X's and the O's."

While Phillips' quote is still used to extol successful coaches, that type of assessment has never really translated well to athletes on the field of play[1]. Max Scherzer can't pick up his opponent's bat and hit his own pitching. Steph Curry can't give another player his own 3-point shots and beat them with their 2-point shots. In individual sports, similar debates have always been hypothetical. It's impossible

---

1. You don't have to limit this discussion to the realm of sports. Warren Buffett can't take my stock portfolio, give me his, and do better. But if he's up for a challenge ...

to know how well John McEnroe could have returned his own serve with Andre Agassi's ground strokes. Of course, the same has always been true of golf – until Mark Broadie came along and changed the way we evaluate golfers and think about their skill sets.

The PGA Tour began collecting individual shot data, with laser precision, at a majority of its sponsored events in 2004. Known as the ShotLink System, within a few years the PGA had data on hundreds of golfers, thousands of rounds and millions of shots. Broadie, a professor at Columbia University who'd previously developed his own database of amateurs' golf shots, began studying the PGA's data and eventually created the Strokes Gained framework which forms the underpinning for all of today's advanced analytics work on the PGA Tour.

Strokes Gained is an elegant creation because it's a zero-sum calculation for every professional golfer on Tour that measures each golfer's performance against his fellow pros. If a golfer's drive on the first tee results in a quarter-stroke gained, then every other golfer in the field will have a fraction-of-a-stroke lost adding to a quarter-stroke. The same logic applies to approach shots, play around the green and putting. It's calculated for every hole in every tournament with ShotLink capabilities (more on that later) so that by the end of the Tour season, everyone who played in a PGA Tour event has Strokes Gained data for the year.

For instance, here is the raw[2] Strokes Gained data for the 2017–2018 season[3], for Justin Rose, the Fed Ex Cup champion and #1 ranked player in the world at the end of the Tour season, and Scott

2. "Raw" for this publication, refers to data unadjusted for strength of field.

3. Traditionally overseeing a sport with calendar-year seasons, the PGA Tour switched to a wrap-around format in the fall of 2013. Therefore, a PGA Tour golfer's season essentially ran October-September from 2013 through last year. Starting this season, the golf year ends in August. Still, going forward, I will refer to the '17-'18 season as the 2018 season, the '16-'17 season as 2017 and so on.

Piercy, a 40-year-old journeyman with four career wins, roughly representing the average PGA touring pro in 2018:

	SG Off the Tee	SG Approach Shots	SG Around Green	SG Putting	SG Total
JR	28.21	21.01	19.79	23.85	92.86
SP	14.18	37.24	3.54	-37.82	17.14

In analytics circles, Strokes Gained is what's known as a counting stat, accumulated with play. Because not all golfers play the same amount of rounds in a year, for a better comparison, the raw Strokes Gained figures are converted to rate stats. This is done by simply dividing total Strokes Gained by the number of rounds played. Rose's Strokes Gained were amassed over 49 rounds while Piercy's totals reflect 64 rounds played, resulting in the following SG/Round figures:

	SG Off the Tee	SG Approach Shots	SG Around Green	SG Putting	SG Total
JR	.576	.429	.404	.487	1.895
SP	.222	.582	.055	-.591	0.268

Viewed in this way, we can say that Justin Rose, the world's #1 ranked player on Tour after the 2018 season, was about 1.63 strokes better than the average touring pro[4] in 2018.

---

4. Since Strokes Gained for all golfers add to zero, you'd expect the "average" PGA pro to have very close to zero SG for the year. In fact, Jhonattan Vegas is that golfer for 2018. However, similar to the concept of Replacement Player (0 WAR) vs. Average Player (2.0 WAR) in Major League Baseball, the average Touring Pro on the PGA Tour, defined here as someone who plays at least 40 rounds during a season, is roughly a quarter-stroke better than the average golfer across all events. That's because there are many amateurs, senior Tour players, and fringe, feeder-Tour pros who get to play in PGA Tour events over the course of a season, and, results-wise they are all well below the level of PGA Touring Pros. Among the more than 600 golfers who played in a PGA event in 2018, 200 or so qualified as Touring Pros. In 2018, Scott Piercy was an average Touring Pro.

For context, a 1.63–stroke-per-round difference in skill is enormous. In theory, a professional golfer that much better than his competitor would win a 4-round match more than 75% of the time. (For sports bettors reading this, it roughly converts to a fair market of – 383/+383 for a Rose vs. Piercy tournament match-up bet, where ties are graded as pushes.) Interestingly, theory played out exactly as expected in 2018. Rose and Piercy entered the same tournament nine times and Rose had the better score in seven events, or 78% of the time.

Now, let's turn back the clock just over a decade to 2007, the first year of the Fed Ex playoffs. Tiger Woods won the inaugural Fed Ex Cup and seven tournaments in 2007, including his 13th major, the 2007 PGA Championship. Here are the Strokes Gained per round figures for Tiger and his long-time rival, Phil Mickelson, for the 2007 season:

	SG Off the Tee	SG Approach Shots	SG Around Green	SG Putting	SG Total
TW	.624	1.653	.103	.712	3.092
PM	.328	.614	.499	.156	1.597

In 2007, Tiger Woods was essentially 1.5 strokes better per round than Phil Mickelson, similar to Rose's performance margin over Piercy last year. Although both Woods and Rose were the top-ranked players at the end of each season, the similarities end there. That's because unlike Scott Piercy, Phil Mickelson wasn't an average touring pro in 2007; no, he was the second-best golfer in the world! Mickelson won three tournaments that year, including The Players Championship, yet he was nearly as inferior to Woods as Piercy currently is to Rose. Look closer at the Strokes Gained components of their skills in 2007, and the words of Bum Phillips can't help but echo in your head. In creating a one-and-a-half stroke margin between the next best player in the world, Tiger excelled in all three areas of getting the golf ball into the hole. That is, driving the ball (SG Off the Tee), getting the ball on the green, excluding drives (SG Approach + SG

Around Green) and Putting (SG Putting). Here's Woods' margin of superiority over Mickelson in those three categories:

SG Off the Tee	SG Approach Shots/ Around Green	SG Putting	SG Total
.296	.643	.556	1.495

As a result, you can make the following astounding conclusion: Tiger Woods could give Phil Mickelson his drives, play Phil's instead and still beat him. (He'd theoretically win by .903 strokes per round, as his .296 SG off the tee would become − .296, reducing his overall advantage of 1.495 by .592.) Or, if Phil would prefer, they could swap skills with the irons and Tiger would still be better by .209 strokes a round. Or they could play their own balls to the green and then switch putting skills and Tiger would still win by an average of .383 strokes a round. Not to put too fine a point on it, but this is comparing Tiger *to the second-best player in the world*. We can't know for sure if Jack Nicklaus, Sam Snead or Ben Hogan were ever that much better than their counterparts, but it's a fairly safe bet that we'll never be able to say in the future what we can say about Tiger in 2007: No matter who you were on Tour, Tiger could take his drive and beat you with your drive, or he could take your drive and beat you with his. Or, you could substitute "approach" or "putt" for "drive" and the conclusion wouldn't change.

Lest you think 2007 was an outlier year for Tiger in which he reached a level of excellence that marked a non-repeatable pinnacle of his performance, here's a listing of Tiger's Strokes Gained per round in the ShotLink era, excluding the injury-marred years from 2014-2017:

2004:   2.382

2005:   2.401

2006:   3.443

2007:   3.092

2008:   3.815

2009:   3.189
2010:   0.139
2011:   0.796
2012:   2.310
2013:   2.064

.

.

2018:   1.651

As measured by Strokes Gained, 2007 actually represented Tiger's *worst* year in the four-year stretch from 2006-2009. And even *that* table doesn't tell the entire story of Tiger's excellence. During this time, the PGA didn't collect ShotLink data at any of the tournaments it didn't oversee, which included all four majors as well as a handful of other foreign-based or multi-course events. As such, Strokes Gained data is only compiled over what's known as "measured rounds." Recalling our 2018 example of Justin Rose and Scott Piercy, their measured rounds may have only been 49 and 64 rounds respectively, but they actually played 66 and 80 rounds in stroke-play events on the PGA Tour last year. Although we have no way of knowing the Strokes Gained components of a round that is not measured by ShotLink, we can very easily determine any golfer's total Strokes Gained for a round or tournament, just by comparing his score to the average of all the other competitors. Using that data, here's another look at Tiger Woods' career, expressed in Strokes Gained per round, from the year he turned pro in 1996, again excluding the injury-marred years from 2014-2017.

	Measured SG/Rd	Overall SG/Rd
1996:		1.401
1997:		2.100
1998:		2.069
1999:		2.938

2000:		3.827
2001:		2.460
2002:		3.002
2003:		2.825
2004:	2.382	2.409
2005:	2.401	2.683
2006:	3.443	3.374
2007:	3.092	3.206
2008:	3.815	3.761
2009:	3.189	3.045
2010:	0.139	0.971
2011:	0.796	0.926
2012:	2.310	2.243
2013:	2.064	2.083
.	.	
.	.	
2018:	1.651	1.568

Two things to note here: 1) In years where his overall Strokes Gained per round are greater than his Strokes Gained per round in measured rounds (e.g. 2004) it means Tiger played better in the majors (and other unmeasured events/rounds) than he did during ShotLink tournaments and 2) Tiger's +3.827 Strokes Gained per round performance in 2000 is almost certainly the greatest season of golf anyone has ever had.

That brings us to the second example of Tiger's otherworldly dominance – The Streak.

If you're a fairly hard-core golf fan and you hear the words "Tiger Woods" and "streak" you'd probably assume it refers to Tiger's Cuts Made streak. From 1998 to 2005 Tiger made 142 cuts in a row, far surpassing the previous record of 113 held by Byron Nelson. That streak is rightly regarded as "unbreakable" in the same sense as Joe

DiMaggio's 56-game hitting streak[5]. DiMaggio's streak has now stood for 77 years so not all of us will get to see if Tiger's accomplishment goes unchallenged for that long, but given that the longest active cuts-made streak on the PGA Tour at the end of the 2018 season was 11 tournaments, it would be shocking if anyone makes a serious run at 142 in a row in the foreseeable future.

As impressive as Tiger's consecutive cuts-made figure is, there's another streak that occurred during the same time period that's even more incredible. Recall that on the previous page, I mentioned we can determine a golfer's Strokes Gained for any round of golf as long as we have the results of everyone who played that day. In building a database for my forthcoming book, *Tour Guide*, I reconstructed the results of every PGA tour event during the Tiger Woods era, 1996-present[6]. Each round for every golfer had a Strokes Gained calculation, red for negative Strokes Gained, and black for positive. It's important to remember what that represents. A player that has positive Strokes Gained for a round scored better than the average of all players who played that round. For instance, in the 4th round of the 2018 Masters, Patrick Reed shot a 71 while the field averaged 70.49 strokes. Reed is said to have lost, or posted negative Strokes Gained of – 0.51 for the round. It stands as an example of a tournament winner – of a major (!) – not having +SG in all four rounds, which perfectly underscores the magnificence of Tiger's streak.

It may not be obvious at first glance, but not all rounds are created equal because there are some degree-of-difficulty differences

---

5. Interestingly, Woods' cuts made streak is 26% higher than Nelson's second-best effort, and DiMaggio's 56-game streak is 27% higher than Pete Rose's 44-game hitting streak, the closest anyone has come to equaling the Yankee Clipper.

6. There are some minor considerations that are addressed in the book that don't have any bearing on the discussion that follows. However, note that I have not been able to locate the scores of golfers who failed to make the cut in 1996 and 1997 tournaments that are now defunct. (e.g. BellSouth Classic.) Additionally, multi-course events (e.g. AT&T Classic at Pebble Beach) create some very minor distortions in my data.

in recording positive Strokes Gained in a round. For instance, it's marginally harder to record positive Strokes Gained in the third or fourth round of a tournament with a cut because, logically, a high percentage of weaker golfers have been weeded out after two rounds. Similarly, in an invitation-only, elite, small-field tournament such as the Tour Championship, it's more difficult to "beat the field" than it is in other tournaments. But the differences in the benchmark, fractions of a stroke per round, are probably smaller than you think.

As I moved forward chronologically from 1996, I began to notice a string of black in Tiger Woods' ledger. From the third round of 1999's WGC-NEC Invitational, Tiger posted positive Strokes Gained every round through the rest of the year, 14 rounds in total. Tiger happened to be in the midst of the greatest tournament run of his career, winning 9 of the 11 stroke-play event tournaments he entered and his consecutive rounds with positive Strokes Gained ("+SG") continued into the 2000 season. Now, as you might suspect, entering the results of every single tournament for 20+ years into an Excel spreadsheet is monotonous, time-consuming work, so as a diversion, the streak began to enthrall me. By the time Tiger got to the Masters in 2000, the +SG streak stood at 38 rounds and I actually got excited to see if he could get through the Masters with the streak still alive. I may have remembered if Tiger won a tournament before I began downloading the data, but this became genuine intrigue every time he played. Sure enough, despite not winning the Masters in 2000, the streak stretched to 42 rounds and I began to wonder when it was going to end. Woods, about to begin the Tiger Slam in two months absolutely dominated the next two majors, so I knew the streak would survive the U.S. Open and Open Championship should it get there but what about in between? Well, despite close calls in the first round of the Byron Nelson and the final round of the Western Open (+0.15 SG, the lowest in all of 2000 during the streak) he roared through the rest of the summer and by the time he returned to Akron, OH for the 2000 WGC-NEC Invitational, I was genuinely nervous about the prospect of Tiger going an entire 365-day period without a −SG round. I shouldn't have been though, as Woods again crushed the field. With the 365-day milestone passed and 74-straight +SG rounds completed, only one piece of drama lay unanswered: Could Tiger go an entire PGA Tour season without a −SG round?

There were four tournaments left in the year and with no worse than a top-3 finish at the Canadian Open, the Disney Classic or the Tour Championship, the streak continued on, reaching 86 rounds by the time he teed it up at the Valderrama Golf Club in Spain for the WGC-American Express Championship. Tiger shot an uninspired 71 in the first round, but it was just good enough to pick up .41 strokes on the field. Then he caught fire Friday and Saturday, moving up the leaderboard from 19th-place in the elite, 54-golfer field after the first round, to a tie for fourth-place with 18 holes to play. Tiger shot a 72 in his last round of the 2000 season to finish four strokes back of the winner, Mike Weir, but all I wanted to know was, what did the field shoot? With an average score of 71.63, the field beat Tiger Woods by a fraction of a stroke and his +SG streak ended at 89 rounds. One stroke! On his final round of the 2000 year, with a chance to record what would have positively been the only "perfect season" in the history of the PGA Tour, Tiger Woods fell one stroke short. Aaaaaaaaaargggh! More than 17 years after the fact, I was crushed his streak ended in that manner.

I spent so much time on the golf course at Stanford University from 1994-1996 while I was getting my MBA, that when people used to ask me what I learned in business school, I'd tell them two things: 1) A dollar today is worth more than a dollar tomorrow and 2) Don't use a driver off the 4th tee. As a result of that extended time on the Stanford golf course, I've met Tiger Woods a number of times as those were the same two years that he attended Stanford. Infamously among my friends, I even turned down the opportunity to interview Tiger for a piece in the student newspaper because, having just been given a column, I thought the assignment was better suited for a reporter, not a columnist[7]. Yet, as I marveled at this accomplishment, I thought that if I were to meet him again today, the only thing I'd want to talk to him about is "the streak." What does he remember about the fourth-round in Valderrama? Did he have any idea the streak existed? Does he even know it today?

It turns out the answer to the last question is yes, he does know about it and the reason he does is that the godfather of all golf data, Mark Broadie knows about it. I don't know the process that led Professor Broadie to uncover the streak, but in a 2015 piece for *Golf Magazine*[8], he discussed what he described as a "beat-the-field" streak. Tiger didn't know of its existence until then, and neither did anyone else. Still unanswered in my mind though, is what happened in the fourth-round of the streak buster? I can't find a scorecard so I don't know how the round played out or if there was an unfortunate bogey on the final hole.

The consecutive cuts-made streak is amazing because, in essence, it means that Tiger went 142 tournaments in a row without having a "blow-up" round on a Thursday or Friday. But think about what the consecutive +SG streak means. It more or less means Tiger went 89 rounds in a row without having a blow-up *hole*! I can't imagine we'll see that level of consistent excellence ever again on the PGA tour.

---

7. If you're among those who have read my baseball content over the years and thought, "this guy's an idiot" always remember, you don't know the half of it.

8. Golf.com/tour-and-news/tiger-woods-consecutive-rounds-streak-might-be-better-joe-dimaggios

CHAPTER 2

Tiger Woods is Even
Better than You Think, Part II

Using the most popular golfer in the world's excellence made for an easy introduction to the Strokes Gained methodology for those who may be unfamiliar with the concept. However, this book is largely a Masters preview, so before we dive into hole-by-hole and golfer-by-golfer, Masters-specific data, let's use Tiger Woods one more time as a way to introduce you to a nuance of Augusta National.

Having spent years diving deeply into sabermetrics and writing something approaching a million words analyzing baseball analytics in my book, *Trading Bases*, in my blog, and on the pages of ESPN. com, I've developed a pretty good ability to detect "announcer bullshit." That's true, actually, for anyone who has a working knowledge of baseball's analytics frontier, and no one has ever done a better job of calling out faulty announcer logic than the trio of guys who created the *Fire Joe Morgan* blog. Now that golf has its own analytics database, almost every telecast provides a helping of commentator fodder, usually from ex-golfers, that borders on the inane. Johnny Miller is rightly regarded as one of the best televised golf commentators of all time, but when he says something like, "Tiger should make that putt 90% of the time" after Woods misses an eight-foot putt as he did during an event last season, I want to slam golf tees into my ear drums[9].

Similarly, the Golf Channel's Brandel Chamblee sure *sounds* like he knows as much about the golf swing and the historical origins of certain swing elements as anyone alive, but when he makes proclamations which can be supported or refuted with a look at the data . . . well, let's examine one in particular. Referring to the well-known superstition that no golfer who has won Augusta National's Par 3 contest held on the eve of the Masters tournament, has ever gone on to win the Masters, Chamblee has said, "You don't want to win the Par 3 contest on Wednesday, but you damn well better win the Par 5 contest starting Thursday."

That sentiment goes hand-in-hand with a veiled criticism of Tiger Woods, or at least an explanation for his dominance designed to mildly diminish his accomplishments. For instance, over the years golf fans have almost certainly read or heard some variation of the following: "In his early years," referring to the Masters, "Tiger was playing a par-68 golf course while it was par-72 for everyone else." Or, in a way that suggests even if he were to bring his age-24, year 2000 performance to the PGA Tour these days, Tiger "wouldn't dominate because he can't overpower the far-better field of players that exists today." Without in any way disputing that today's top golfers are better, and most notably *better younger*, as a whole than Tour players of the last generation, there are a lot of ways to debunk the idea that it would have made a difference in Tiger's overall success. I'll dive into those topics in my forthcoming book, but for the rest of this chapter, let's confine the discussion to Tiger at Augusta.

When Woods won his first Masters at the age of 21 in 1997, he

---

9. One of the immutable tenants of Mark Broadie's work is that for pro golfers, an eight-foot putt is a 50/50 proposition and owing to bell curves and standard deviations, no golfer can ever hope to achieve a greater than 60% make-rate over time.

truly did overpower the golf course and the field. It only took Colin Montgomerie, then the third-ranked golfer in the world, playing one round with Tiger at the Masters to go from hopeful challenger, eager to take on the young pro, to demoralized foe and true believer. Montgomerie began the third round of the 1997 Masters in second place and as such was paired with Woods, the tournament leader after 36 holes, for their third rounds. When he spoke to reporters afterwards, the normally cocky and brash Scotsman stood 12 strokes behind Woods and was asked about the prospect of Woods blowing his nine-stroke lead. Knowing what he'd just witnessed first-hand he said, "There's no chance humanly possible." Reporters reminded him that just a year before Greg Norman had blown a seemingly insurmountable lead on Sunday, to which Montgomerie replied, "Greg Norman's not Tiger Woods."

Lest you forget, the player Montgomerie slammed with that burn, Greg Norman, was the number one-ranked player in the world at the time!

So, knowing that Woods obliterated the field and the course – Rick Reilly noted in his deadline-piece for *Sports Illustrated* that Woods drove the ball 25 yards further than his closest competitor and that he was hitting "a wedge into the 500-yard Par 5 15th hole – for his **second** shot" – you would probably expect very different tournament results if all of the Par 5s were removed from the competition.

Think about what that means for a second. Over the course of 72 holes, there are 16, par-5 holes which make up 22% of the holes and an even larger 28% of the strokes for par (20 out of 72.) So if you remove those holes and shorten the tournament, you'd not only be adding more randomness to the event (similar to Princeton always trying to shorten a basketball game versus superior opponents during the Pete Carril-era) but you'd also be removing Woods' greatest perceived skill versus the entire field. Because you'd be removing the "Par 5 contest" entirely from the tournament, you'd be neutralizing Tiger, right?

Well, here's what the top of 1997 Masters Leaderboard looked like:

Woods	−18
Kite	−6
Tolles	−5
Watson	−4
Rocca	−3
Stankowski	−3
Sluman	−2
Couples	−2
Love III	−2
Leonard	−2
Langer	−2

Here's what it looked like with all the Par 5 holes removed:

Woods	−5
Kite	−4
Tolles	+1
Watson	+1
Rocca	+3
Sluman	+3
Leonard	+3
Stankowski	+4
Couples	+6
Langer	+6
Love III	+8

Looking at the before-and-after leaderboards, you can see Tiger did indeed win the "Par 5 tournament" in 1997 as his score dropped the most (13 strokes) with the removal of the Par 5 results. But he also won the "Par 3 tournament" having been the only one of the leaders to shoot even par over four rounds on the 16 par 3s. And note, he still would have won the 1997 Masters if it were only 52 holes consisting entirely of Par 3s and Par 4s!

What about his other three Masters victories? In 2001, his two-stroke victory would have turned into a one-stroke loss to Mark Calcavecchia with the removal of the Par 5s, but his position atop the leaderboard in 2002 and 2005 would not have changed with the omission of the Par 5s.

Look, Chamblee's assertion in and of itself is not incorrect. Further, if he meant it as a prediction for the 2018 Masters, as we'll see in a later chapter, he nailed it. It's factual that you *do* have to score well on the Par 5s to win at Augusta because that's the most common place to gain strokes versus par. But if someone uses that logic in any way to detract from Tiger's excellence at Augusta, or to dismiss the importance of performance on the Par 3 holes, remember that in his four wins, he only once won the "Par 5 contest." Further, removing the Par 5s altogether would have only cost him a single green jacket, which again, is astounding when you realize that stipulation reduces each round of the tournament to a par-52, 14-hole contest.

As the PGA Tour has never been permitted to install its ShotLink technology at Augusta National, looking at old scorecards, as I did to crunch the Par 3 and Par 5 data above, has been the only way to analyze golfer performance at the Masters.

Until now, that is.

In the pages that follow, you'll learn not just who won the "Par 3" and "Par 5 contests" over the course of the 2018 Masters and if that translated into overall success, but you'll find out how exactly Patrick Reed beat the field, why neither the best driver of the ball all tournament nor the best iron player won, and why, for last year at least, Tony Finau set the gold standard for putting success during a single round of golf at Augusta National.

All of that and more are presented in the Strokes Gained format with which today's analytics-inclined golf fan is well-acquainted. Without further ado, the 2018 Masters Strokes Gained report and the 2019 Masters preview . . . .

CHAPTER 3

The 2018 Strokes Gained Report

I f you opened up the sports section of your local newspaper on Monday, April 9, 2018, you almost certainly could find a "box score" of the Masters Tournament completed the day before, in the form of a leaderboard. It probably looked something like this:

2018 Masters Results, Traditional View

Finish	Golfer	To Par	Rd 1	Rd 2	Rd 3	Rd 4	Total
1	Patrick Reed	-15	69	66	67	71	273
2	Rickie Fowler	-14	70	72	65	67	274
3	Jordan Spieth	-13	66	74	71	64	275
4	Jon Rahm	-11	75	68	65	69	277
T5	Henrik Stenson	-9	69	70	70	70	279
T5	Rory McIlroy	-9	69	71	65	74	279
T5	Cameron Smith	-9	71	72	70	66	279
T5	Bubba Watson	-9	73	69	68	69	279
9	Marc Leishman	-8	70	67	73	70	280
T10	Dustin Johnson	-7	73	68	71	69	281
T10	Tony Finau	-7	68	74	73	66	281
T12	Louis Oosthuizen	-6	71	71	71	69	282
T12	Charley Hoffman	-6	69	73	73	67	282
T12	Justin Rose	-6	72	70	71	69	282
T15	Russell Henley	-5	73	72	71	67	283
T15	Paul Casey	-5	74	75	69	65	283

T17	Justin Thomas	-4	74	67	70	73	284
T17	Tommy Fleetwood	-4	72	72	66	74	284
19	Hideki Matsuyama	-3	73	71	72	69	285
T20	Francesco Molinari	-2	72	74	70	70	286
T20	Jason Day	-2	75	71	69	71	286
T20	Webb Simpson	-2	76	73	70	67	286
T20	Jimmy Walker	-2	73	71	71	71	286
T24	Branden Grace	-1	73	73	74	67	287
T24	Si Woo Kim	-1	75	73	68	71	287
T24	Bernd Wiesberger	-1	70	73	72	72	287
T24	Adam Hadwin	-1	69	75	72	71	287
T28	Ryan Moore	E	74	72	72	70	288
T28	Satoshi Kodaira	E	71	74	71	72	288
T28	Matt Kuchar	E	68	75	72	73	288
T28	Kevin Kisner	E	72	75	69	72	288
T32	Adam Scott	+1	75	73	70	71	289
T32	Hao Tong Li	+1	69	76	72	72	289
T32	Tiger Woods	+1	73	75	72	69	289
T32	Daniel Berger	+1	73	74	71	71	289
T36	Zach Johnson	+2	70	74	74	72	290
T36	Phil Mickelson	+2	70	79	74	67	290
T38	Bryson DeChambeau	+3	74	74	72	71	291
T38	Rafa Cabrera Bello	+3	69	76	74	72	291
T38	Bernhard Langer	+3	74	74	71	72	291
T38	Fred Couples	+3	72	74	73	72	291
T38	Jhonattan Vegas	+3	77	69	72	73	291
T38	Matthew Fitzpatrick	+3	75	74	67	75	291
T44	Kiradech Aphibarnrat	+4	79	70	72	71	292
T44	Tyrrell Hatton	+4	74	75	73	70	292
T44	Brian Harman	+4	73	74	76	69	292
T44	Ian Poulter	+4	74	75	74	69	292
48	Martin Kaymer	+6	74	73	74	73	294
49	Vijay Singh	+7	71	74	79	71	295
T50	Xander Schauffele	+8	71	78	72	75	296
T50	Doug Ghim	+8	72	76	74	74	296

52	Kyle Stanley	+9	72	74	75	76	297
53	Chez Reavie	+10	76	71	75	76	298
CUT	Charl Schwartzel		72	78			150
CUT	Jason Dufner		73	77			150
CUT	Sandy Lyle		74	76			150
CUT	Jose Maria Olazabal		74	76			150
CUT	Brendan Steele		76	75			151
CUT	Patrick Cantlay		75	76			151
CUT	Danny Willett		75	76			151
CUT	Thomas Pieters		73	78			151
.							
.							
CUT	Harry Ellis		86	80			166

For space reasons, I've omitted a number of the 34 golfers who missed the cut, but for all 53 golfers who made the cut at last year's Masters, you see their results presented in a format with which all casual golf fans are familiar. In fact, if you removed the scores from all rounds except the 4th, it would present the same information CBS shows during its telecast.

The traditional leaderboard tells you how everyone finished and their relation to par, but there's not a lot of additional insight to be gleaned. You might look at last year's board and note that in posting a 64 on Sunday, Jordan Spieth shot the best round of the tournament or recall that Patrick Reed's – 15 probably stacks up well with the winning scores in recent Masters, but there's not much else to learn from this presentation of results.

However, now let's look at the same leaderboard presented in a Strokes Gained format, instead of overall strokes taken.

2018 Masters Results, Strokes Gained View

Finish	Golfer	To Par	SG:Rd 1	SG:Rd 2	SG:Rd 3	SG:Rd 4	SG:Total
1	Patrick Reed	−15	4.79	8.56	4.26	−0.51	17.11
2	Rickie Fowler	−14	3.79	2.56	6.26	3.49	16.11
3	Jordan Spieth	−13	7.79	0.56	0.26	6.49	15.11
4	Jon Rahm	−11	−1.21	6.56	6.26	1.49	13.11
T5	Henrik Stenson	−9	4.79	4.56	1.26	0.49	11.11
T5	Rory McIlroy	−9	4.79	3.56	6.26	−3.51	11.11
T5	Cameron Smith	−9	2.79	2.56	1.26	4.49	11.11
T5	Bubba Watson	−9	0.79	5.56	3.26	1.49	11.11
9	Marc Leishman	−8	3.79	7.56	−1.74	0.49	10.11
T10	Dustin Johnson	−7	0.79	6.56	0.26	1.49	9.11
T10	Tony Finau	−7	5.79	0.56	−1.74	4.49	9.11
T12	Louis Oosthuizen	−6	2.79	3.56	0.26	1.49	8.11
T12	Charley Hoffman	−6	4.79	1.56	0.26	3.49	8.11
T12	Justin Rose	−6	1.79	4.56	2.26	1.49	8.11
T15	Russell Henley	−5	0.79	2.56	1.26	3.49	7.11
T15	Paul Casey	−5	−0.21	−0.44	5.26	5.49	7.11
T17	Justin Thomas	−4	−0.21	7.56	−0.74	−2.51	6.11
T17	Tommy Fleetwood	−4	1.79	2.56	1.26	−3.51	6.11
19	Hideki Matsuyama	−3	0.79	3.56	2.26	1.49	5.11
T20	Francesco Molinari	−2	1.79	0.56	1.26	0.49	4.11
T20	Jason Day	−2	−1.21	3.56	0.26	−0.51	4.11
T20	Webb Simpson	−2	−2.21	1.56	−2.74	3.49	4.11
T20	Jimmy Walker	−2	0.79	3.56	3.26	−0.51	4.11
T24	Branden Grace	−1	0.79	1.56	−0.74	−1.51	3.11
T24	Si Woo Kim	−1	−1.21	1.56	−0.74	−0.51	3.11
T24	Bernd Wiesberger	−1	3.79	1.56	−0.74	0.49	3.11
T24	Adam Hadwin	−1	4.79	−0.44	0.26	−1.51	3.11
T28	Ryan Moore	E	−0.21	2.56	−0.74	−2.51	2.11
T28	Satoshi Kodaira	E	2.79	0.56	0.26	−1.51	2.11
T28	Matt Kuchar	E	5.79	−0.44	−0.74	−2.51	2.11
T28	Kevin Kisner	E	1.79	−0.44	2.26	−1.51	2.11
T32	Adam Scott	+1	−1.21	1.56	1.26	−0.51	1.11
T32	Hao Tong Li	+1	4.79	−1.44	−0.74	−1.51	1.11
T32	Tiger Woods	+1	0.79	−0.44	−0.74	1.49	1.11
T32	Daniel Berger	+1	0.79	0.56	0.26	−0.51	1.11
T36	Zach Johnson	+2	3.79	0.56	−2.74	−1.51	0.11

T36	Phil Mickelson	+2	3.79	-4.44	-2.74	3.49	0.11
T38	Bryson DeChambeau	+3	-0.21	0.56	-0.74	-0.51	-0.89
T38	Rafa Cabrera Bello	+3	4.79	-1.44	-2.74	-1.51	-0.89
T38	Bernhard Langer	+3	-0.21	0.56	0.26	-1.51	-0.89
T38	Fred Couples	+3	1.79	0.56	-1.74	-1.51	-0.89
T38	Jhonattan Vegas	+3	-3.21	5.56	-0.74	-2.51	-0.89
T38	Matthew Fitzpatrick	+3	-1.21	0.56	4.26	-4.51	-0.89
T44	Kiradech Aphibarnrat	+4	-5.21	4.56	-0.74	-0.51	-1.89
T44	Tyrrell Hatton	+4	-0.21	-0.44	-1.74	0.49	-1.89
T44	Brian Harman	+4	0.79	0.56	-4.74	1.49	-1.89
T44	Ian Poulter	+4	-0.21	-0.44	-2.74	1.49	-1.89
48	Martin Kaymer	+6	-0.21	1.56	-2.74	-2.51	-3.89
49	Vijay Singh	+7	2.79	0.56	-7.74	-0.51	-4.89
T50	Xander Schauffele	+8	2.79	-3.44	-0.74	-4.51	-5.89
T50	Doug Ghim	+8	1.79	-1.44	-2.74	-3.51	-5.89
52	Kyle Stanley	+9	1.79	0.56	-3.74	-5.51	-6.89
53	Chez Reavie	+10	-2.21	3.56	-3.74	-5.51	-7.89
CUT	Charl Schwartzel		1.79	-3.44			-1.64
CUT	Jason Dufner		0.79	-2.44			-1.64
CUT	Sandy Lyle		-0.21	-1.44			-1.64
CUT	Jose Maria Olazabal		-0.21	-1.44			-1.64
CUT	Brendan Steele		-2.21	-0.44			-2.64
CUT	Patrick Cantlay		-1.21	-1.44			-2.64
CUT	Danny Willett		-1.21	-1.44			-2.64
CUT	Thomas Pieters		0.79	-3.44			-2.64
.							
.							
CUT	Harry Ellis		-12.21	-5.44			-17.64

Presented in this format, we can start to gain insights into the tournament. First, let's take a step back and discuss what it takes to win a tournament on the PGA Tour, using logic familiar to baseball's sabermetric community.

I wrote individual season team previews for all 30 MLB teams for ESPN from 2015-2017. If you read the write-ups, or watched the accompanying videos, or listened to any of the many podcasts I appeared on, you became familiar with this oft-repeated sentence: If an MLB team truly has playoff aspirations, it'd better have a realistic plan in place to outscore its opponents by 100 runs over the course of the 162-game season.

There are basic sabermetric principles underlying that sentence that we don't need to explore here but we can make this similar statement regarding professional golfers: If you want to win a tournament on the PGA Tour, you'd better have a skill set that allows you to accumulate at least 14 Strokes Gained over four rounds.

Remember, a golfer's Strokes Gained for a round is calculated by subtracting his score from the average score of all the golfers who played that round. Since the field averaged a score of 70.49 in last year's final round, Jordan Spieth's 64 worked out to 6.49 Strokes Gained, which you can see in the table above.

Looking at the far-right column, note that not only did Patrick Reed exceed +14 SG for the tournament but so did Rickie Fowler and Jordan Spieth, suggesting they also played well enough to win the tournament. Enlightened baseball fans know not to penalize a batter for a lack of RBIs because his teammates were rarely on base when he came up, and these days even Cy Young Award voters don't penalize pitchers for a lack of "wins" because that statistic is heavily dependent on the performance of a team's hitters – something not under the pitcher's control. In assigning glory or blame, therefore, to professional golfers based on the number of tournaments, including majors, they win, one needs to be very careful to separate perfor-mance of the golfer under question – something he can control – from performance of his competitors, which he can't[10]. Look again

---

10. I explore this topic of luck and tournament victories much further in my upcoming book and once you've read it, maybe I'll be able to convince you that Jim Furyk was every bit as good a golfer as Phil Mickelson during the decade when they were both at their peak.

at the scoreboard above. Next time you want to criticize Rickie Fowler for having never won a major, remember that he outperformed the field of golfers he faced last year at Augusta by a greater margin *than seven of the last twelve Masters winners* prior to 2018.

There are two other items of note when the results of the 2018 Masters are presented in Strokes Gained form: 1) Jordan Spieth's 64 on Sunday wasn't the best round of the tournament – in fact it wasn't even *his* best round of the tournament. It may have been the low round, but just as a birdie 2 on a Par 3 isn't as good as an eagle 3 on a Par 5, the low round isn't necessarily the best: *The best round in any tournament is the round that picks up the most ground on the field.* As the Strokes Gained leaderboard shows, Patrick Reed shot the best round of the tournament (on Friday.) 2) With negative Strokes Gained rounds in red, it's immediately noticeable that Reed had –SG on Sunday. That's highly unusual, as winners aren't usually leaking oil prior to donning the green jacket. Of the 22 prior winners spanning the Tiger Woods' era on the PGA tour, the Masters winner averaged +3.68 SG on Sunday and only Trevor Immelman posted –SG (-0.33 SG in 2008.)

While the Strokes Gained format is superior to the traditional scoreboard for understanding performance relative to the field, we still haven't really unlocked why or how each golfer got to his final spot on the leaderboard. For that we need the components of Strokes Gained, and as mentioned earlier, the PGA Tour is not permitted to install its ShotLink equipment at Augusta. So how is it possible, on the pages that follow, for me to present that data to you from the 2018 Masters? Here's the story of the data and my methodology.

The PGA Tour and its technology partner CDW may not be able to install their equipment at the Augusta National Golf Club, but as viewers of the CBS broadcast know, IBM is a sponsor of the Masters. It turns out that when the Masters website launched its Track function a few years ago, it used IBM's technology to provide information on each shot for golfers that mobile or desktop visitors chose to track. If you're crazy enough to do it, you can do what I did – record all 20,420 shots taken at the 2018 Masters in a spreadsheet to form a database.

Once I got the shot information in a database, I turned to the work of Mark Broadie to convert that raw information into Shots Gained data. For instance, in his 2010 paper *Assessing Golfer Performance on the PGA Tour*, which led to his 2014 book *Every Shot Counts*, Broadie assigns a baseline for every shot a PGA Tour player takes whether from the tee, the fairway, the rough, in a recovery situation or on the green. Using that information, it's possible to assign Strokes Gained to every shot in the database. Let's take a look at how Jordan Spieth did on the first hole of the tournament.

The first hole on the course, named Tea Olive for a flowering shrub at Augusta native to Asia yet common to the southeastern United States, is a 445-yard Par 4. According to Broadie's work, PGA pros have an expected score of 4.10 on holes of this length. Spieth hit a 295-yard drive in the fairway, 156 yards from the hole. From there his approach landed on the green, stopping 30 feet from the pin. He missed his birdie putt and made the clean-up, 3-foot putt that remained for par.

Here's how the Strokes Gained methodology graded his work on the hole:

- A 156-yard shot from the fairway should take a pro, on average, 2.88 strokes to get in the hole. Spieth started the hole with an expected score of 4.10. From tee to fairway, his expected score dropped 1.22 strokes. His drive was therefore worth +0.22 SG, or SG:OTT in Strokes Gained shorthand, where OTT stands for "off the tee."

- Broadie's work also tells us that putting from 30 feet away on the green, pros have an expected score of 1.98, which simply means they are very slightly more likely to make a putt from that distance than they are to three-putt. As a result of his approach shot, Spieth actually lost − .1 SG as his spent shot only lowered his expected score by .9 strokes (2.88 − 1.98.) As such, he's credited with −.1 SG:App for his approach shot.

- Finally, his two-putt from 30 feet cost him a miniscule − 0.02 SG:P (2 − 1.98.)

Put it all together and Spieth's Strokes Gained scorecard for first hole looks like this:

SG:OTT	SG:App	SG:P	SG:Tot
0.22	−0.10	−0.02	0.10

Jordan Spieth had +.1 SG on Hole 1 of the first round of the Masters, comprised of three different skill-based components. Do that for every golfer, on every hole, and by the end of the tournament you'll get this Expanded Strokes Gained Leaderboard[11]:

2018 Masters Results, Expanded Strokes Gained View

Finish	Golfer	To Par	SG: Rd 1	SG: Rd 2	SG: Rd 3	SG: Rd 4	SG: Total	SG: OTT	SG: A/AG	SG:P
1	Patrick Reed	-15	4.79	8.56	4.26	-0.51	17.11	3.35	5.21	8.56
2	Rickie Fowler	-14	3.79	2.56	6.26	3.49	16.11	0.86	6.72	8.53
3	Jordan Spieth	-13	7.79	0.56	0.26	6.49	15.11	-0.37	13.07	2.41
4	Jon Rahm	-11	-1.21	6.56	6.26	1.49	13.11	5.94	2.58	4.59
T5	Henrik Stenson	-9	4.79	4.56	1.26	0.49	11.11	0.71	9.8	0.60
T5	Rory McIlroy	-9	4.79	3.56	6.26	-3.51	11.11	5.82	4.15	1.14
T5	Cameron Smith	-9	2.79	2.56	1.26	4.49	11.11	-0.68	9.53	2.25
T5	Bubba Watson	-9	0.79	5.56	3.26	1.49	11.11	8.92	-0.22	2.42
9	Marc Leishman	-8	3.79	7.56	-1.74	0.49	10.11	-1.27	7.33	4.05
T10	Dustin Johnson	-7	0.79	6.56	0.26	1.49	9.11	3.78	5.69	-0.36

---

11. To complete the task, you also have to normalize every SG component of every hole so that everything sums to zero, but in practice those adjustments result in miniscule changes.

T10	Tony Finau	-7	5.79	0.56	-1.74	4.49	9.11	0.35	3.16	5.60
T12	Louis Oosthuizen	-6	2.79	3.56	0.26	1.49	8.11	1.45	6.54	0.12
T12	Charley Hoffman	-6	4.79	1.56	0.26	3.49	8.11	-0.52	7.97	0.67
T12	Justin Rose	-6	1.79	4.56	2.26	1.49	8.11	5.20	0.77	2.14
T15	Russell Henley	-5	0.79	2.56	1.26	3.49	7.11	1.15	5.42	0.55
T15	Paul Casey	-5	-0.21	-0.44	5.26	5.49	7.11	-1.72	2.72	6.10
T17	Justin Thomas	-4	-0.21	7.56	-0.74	-2.51	6.11	2.57	5.37	-1.83
T17	Tommy Fleetwood	-4	1.79	2.56	1.26	-3.51	6.11	2.68	0.73	2.70
19	Hideki Matsuyama	-3	0.79	3.56	2.26	1.49	5.11	3.58	1.31	0.22
T20	Francesco Molinari	-2	1.79	0.56	1.26	0.49	4.11	3.31	5.40	-4.60
T20	Jason Day	-2	-1.21	3.56	0.26	-0.51	4.11	1.15	2.14	0.82
T20	Webb Simpson	-2	-2.21	1.56	-2.74	3.49	4.11	-0.38	1.44	3.05
T20	Jimmy Walker	-2	0.79	3.56	3.26	-0.51	4.11	-3.72	4.69	3.14
T24	Branden Grace	-1	0.79	1.56	-0.74	-1.51	3.11	-1.96	9.78	-4.71
T24	Si Woo Kim	-1	-1.21	1.56	-0.74	-0.51	3.11	0.08	4.96	-1.93
T24	Bernd Wiesberger	-1	3.79	1.56	-0.74	0.49	3.11	-0.58	5.49	-1.80
T24	Adam Hadwin	-1	4.79	-0.44	0.26	-1.51	3.11	-2.81	4.03	1.89
T28	Ryan Moore	E	-0.21	2.56	-0.74	-2.51	2.11	0.16	3.38	-1.42
T28	Satoshi Kodaira	E	2.79	0.56	0.26	-1.51	2.11	-0.80	3.44	-0.52
T28	Matt Kuchar	E	5.79	-0.44	-0.74	-2.51	2.11	-2.27	-1.61	6.00
T28	Kevin Kisner	E	1.79	-0.44	2.26	-1.51	2.11	1.54	-8.25	8.82
T32	Adam Scott	+1	-1.21	1.56	1.26	-0.51	1.11	5.25	0.92	-5.06
T32	Hao Tong Li	+1	4.79	-1.44	-0.74	-1.51	1.11	-0.90	5.30	-3.29
T32	Tiger Woods	+1	0.79	-0.44	-0.74	1.49	1.11	1.66	-0.03	-0.52
T32	Daniel Berger	+1	0.79	0.56	0.26	-0.51	1.11	3.99	-7.46	4.58
T36	Zach Johnson	+2	3.79	0.56	-2.74	-1.51	0.11	-2.55	1.59	1.07
T36	Phil Mickelson	+2	3.79	-4.44	-2.74	3.49	0.11	-4.12	-0.35	4.58
T38	Bryson DeChambeau	+3	-0.21	0.56	-0.74	-0.51	-0.89	4.28	0.57	-5.74
T38	Rafa Cabrera Bello	+3	4.79	-1.44	-2.74	-1.51	-0.89	0.37	2.23	-3.48
T38	Bernhard Langer	+3	-0.21	0.56	0.26	-1.51	-0.89	0.04	1.06	-1.98
T38	Fred Couples	+3	1.79	0.56	-1.74	-1.51	-0.89	-2.18	0.61	0.67
T38	Jhonattan Vegas	+3	-3.21	5.56	-0.74	-2.51	-0.89	0.03	-2.58	1.66
T38	Matthew Fitzpatrick	+3	-1.21	0.56	4.26	-4.51	-0.89	0.61	-5.79	4.29
T44	Kiradech Aphibarnrat	+4	-5.21	4.56	-0.74	-0.51	-1.89	-0.57	-0.59	-0.73
T44	Tyrrell Hatton	+4	-0.21	-0.44	-1.74	0.49	-1.89	0.12	-1.57	-0.44
T44	Brian Harman	+4	0.79	0.56	-4.74	1.49	-1.89	-0.78	-1.66	0.55

T44	Ian Poulter	+4	−0.21	−0.44	−2.74	1.49	−1.89	−0.91	−2.68	1.71
48	Martin Kaymer	+6	−0.21	1.56	−2.74	−2.51	−3.89	−3.49	1.52	−1.93
49	Vijay Singh	+7	2.79	0.56	−7.74	−0.51	−4.89	−2.77	−0.10	−2.01
T50	Xander Schauffele	+8	2.79	−3.44	−0.74	−4.51	−5.89	0.92	−2.55	−4.27
T50	Doug Ghim	+8	1.79	−1.44	−2.74	−3.51	−5.89	−3.03	−2.71	−0.15
52	Kyle Stanley	+9	1.79	0.56	−3.74	−5.51	−6.89	−0.47	2.92	−9.34
53	Chez Reavie	+10	−2.21	3.56	−3.74	−5.51	−7.89	−0.70	−5.93	−1.26
CUT	Charl Schwartzel		1.79	−3.44			−1.64	−0.12	−1.93	0.40
CUT	Jason Dufner		0.79	−2.44			−1.64	−3.63	0.04	1.94
CUT	Sandy Lyle		−0.21	−1.44			−1.64	−2.24	−3.18	3.78
CUT	Jose Maria Olazabal		−0.21	−1.44			−1.64	−4.67	−2.11	5.14
CUT	Brendan Steele		−2.21	−0.44			−2.64	1.50	−0.29	−3.85
CUT	Patrick Cantlay		−1.21	−1.44			−2.64	1.06	−0.87	−2.83
CUT	Danny Willett		−1.21	−1.44			−2.64	−1.15	0.09	−1.58
CUT	Thomas Pieters		0.79	−3.44			−2.64	1.37	−3.20	−0.82
.										
.										
CUT	Harry Ellis		−12.21	−5.44			−17.64	−5.31	−7.94	−4.40

By decomposing each golfer's total Strokes Gained into three different skill sets, performance off the tee; approaching the green, including scrambling around the green;[12] and putting, we get a true window into how each golfer performed over the course of the tournament.

While Patrick Reed and Rickie Fowler putted extremely well over the course of four rounds, Jordan Spieth rode spectacular iron play to his top-3 finish. It's been said that the layout of Augusta National suits Bubba Watson's left-handed fade perfectly, and we no longer have to speculate as to the reasons for the two-time winner's Masters success. In fact, we can actually quantify it. Looking at the SG:OTT column, it's clear Watson drove the ball, by far, better than anyone else in the field. However, he simply didn't take advantage of his superior location off the tee compared to his competitors as he finished with a below-average

12. Broadie's work breaks approach shots (which include tee shots on par 3 holes) and scrambling around the green (bunker shots, chips, etc.) into separate skills. His more granular approach is clearly superior, but I merged the two as a concession to manually working with a database of more than 20,000 shots.

reading getting the ball to the green. It's fair to say that if Jordan Spieth could hit his iron shots from Watson's drive location, you're looking at a runaway winner. (Come to think of it, that plan probably wouldn't have worked worse than any of the pairing strategies captain Jim Furyk tried at last fall's Ryder Cup. Sigh.)

It's notable that Patrick Reed didn't actually do anything better than the rest of the field, although his putting over four rounds was close. What really distinguished his performance was the balance of excellence. Reed gained exactly as many strokes on the field getting the ball to the green as he did once he took the putter from his bag.

Balance matters; everyone that finished in the top 20 outpaced the field in at least two of the three areas of skill, and no one that had +SG in all three areas finished outside the top 20. There were some standout performances, both good and bad, for each skill set, so let's take a look at the field's performance by skill set.

CHAPTER 4

Skill Set Leaderboards

Because tee shots on Par 3 holes are classified as approach shots in the Strokes Gained methodology pioneered by Mark Broadie, there are 14 tee shots each round of the Masters that get treated as drives "off the tee." Here are the Top 20 golfers in Strokes Gained, Off the Tee at last year's Masters.

2018 Masters, Top SG:OTT Performers

Rank	Golfer	SG:OTT	Rounds
1	Bubba Watson	8.92	4
2	Jon Rahm	5.94	4
3	Rory McIlroy	5.82	4
4	Adam Scott	5.25	4
5	Justin Rose	5.20	4
6	Bryson DeChambeau	4.28	4
7	Daniel Berger	3.99	4
8	Dustin Johnson	3.78	4
9	Hideki Matsuyama	3.58	4
10	Patrick Reed	3.35	4
11	Francesco Molinari	3.31	4
12	Tommy Fleetwood	2.68	4
13	Justin Thomas	2.57	4
14	Sergio Garcia	2.52	2

15	Yuxin Lin	2.08	2
15	Shubhankar Sharma	1.78	2
17	Tiger Woods	1.66	4
18	Kevin Chappell	1.56	2
19	Kevin Kisner	1.54	4
20	Brendan Steele	1.50	2

At 8.92, Bubba Watson's Strokes Gained Off the Tee were so much better than the rest of the field's, I found myself constantly reconfirming my calculations. But they checked out. Here's the best way to express his excellence driving the ball compared to the rest of the field. Watson hit 47 out of 56 fairways off the tee over the course of the Masters; only Bernhard Langer, with 48, hit more. While both of the former two-time winners of the event were paragons of accuracy, the similarities in their driving results end there. Langer's 56 drives finished a combined 11,086 yards from the pin, or an average of 198 yards away per drive. Watson gained nearly 2,000 more cumulative yards off the tee than Langer, finishing 9,256 yards from the pin, or 165 yards away on average. (In trying to process how good that is, remember the 165-yards-away average includes 16 Par 5 holes out of the 56 drives.)

For the tournament, Watson finished a close second in terms of distance to the hole after drives. Rory McIlroy's drives finished closer to the hole by a cumulative 101 yards compared to Watson's tee shots. The difference is where the ball lay. McIlroy only found the fairway 35 times, which means although they hit their tee shots roughly the same distance, 12 more times than Watson, McIlroy found his ball in a less than ideal location, be it in trees, on pine straw, in a bunker, or in Augusta's "second cut." McIlroy's distance was a weapon, no doubt, and it's why he's 3rd in the above table. But Bubba Watson drove the ball with the accuracy of Bernhard Langer and the power of Rory McIlroy. That's an unbeatable combination off the tee and it's why he led his next-closest competitor by nearly three strokes.

So who were the worst drivers off the tee? That's interesting too, for Mike Weir and Phil Mickelson are left-handed former champions, just like Watson.

2018 Masters, Worst SG:OTT Performers

Rank	Golfer	SG:OTT	Rounds
87	Harry Ellis	-5.31	2
86	Jose Maria Olazabal	-4.67	2
85	Phil Mickelson	-4.12	4
84	Mike Weir	-3.99	2
83	Jimmy Walker	-3.72	4

Of course, as mentioned in a prior chapter, Strokes Gained is a counting stat, accumulated with play, so Mickelson and Jimmy Walker weren't as bad per round as the others, but their inclusion provides quite a contrast over 56 tee shots with those in the first table.

Speaking of that first table, there are five golfers who finished in the top 20 in Strokes Gained Off the Tee, despite missing the cut and only playing two rounds. One of them, the 2017 champion, Sergio Garcia, drove the ball very well but the story of his unsuccessful title defense is contained in the following discussion of iron play.

Here are the Top 20 golfers in Strokes Gained, Approach Shots and Around the Green at last year's Masters.

2018 Masters, Top SG:App/AG Performers

Rank	Golfer	SG:App/AG	Rounds
1	Jordan Spieth	13.07	4
2	Henrik Stenson	9.80	4
3	Branden Grace	9.78	4
4	Cameron Smith	9.53	4
5	Charley Hoffman	7.97	4

6	Marc Leishman	7.33	4
7	Rickie Fowler	6.72	4
8	Louis Oosthuizen	6.54	4
9	Dustin Johnson	5.69	4
10	Bernd Wiesberger	5.49	4
11	Russell Henley	5.42	4
12	Francesco Molinari	5.40	4
13	Justin Thomas	5.37	4
14	Hao Tong Li	5.30	4
15	Patrick Reed	5.21	4
15	Si Woo Kim	4.96	4
17	Jimmy Walker	4.69	4
18	Rory McIlroy	4.15	4
19	Adam Hadwin	4.03	4
20	Satoshi Kodaira	3.44	4

Jordan Spieth posted an unheard of +13 SG:App/AG over his four rounds last year. Recall, +14 SG is the benchmark for winning a tournament and Spieth nearly would have gotten there with just average driving and putting. Although his driving was just short of average, his putting added even more distance versus the field, and when we move to a discussion of putting we'll see what Patrick Reed had to do on the greens to overcome Spieth's superior job of getting the ball on the green. Before we do that though, here's a look at the worst iron play at last year's Masters and the promised look at Garcia's demise.

2018 Masters, Worst SG:App/AG Performers

Rank	Golfer	SG:App/AG	Rounds
87	Sergio Garcia	–14.07	2
86	Matt Parziale	–9.39	2
85	Kevin Kisner	–8.25	4
84	Harry Ellis	–7.94	2
83	Daniel Berger	–7.46	4

No one who witnessed the uncomfortable spectacle of the Spaniard dunking five consecutive shots in the water that fronts the 15th green could help but feel sorry for the defending champion. In carding a 13 on the Par 5 15th hole, Garcia lost − 9.02 Strokes Gained for his work with the irons. That in itself is notable because take away that single hole and Garcia, normally one of the best iron players on Tour, still had − 5.05 SG:App/AG which would have ranked him 77th in the field of 83. We have no way of knowing if Garcia simply gave up after the first-round disaster at 15, but we do know that he played quite poorly on the other 35 holes he did complete.

That's a look at how each golfer in the field did last year in getting his ball on the green. Augusta, with its large fairways and an absence of thick rough, isn't a particularly penal course in terms of driving the ball, and the greens offer sizable targets for approach shots once they're in sight. The size of the greens are deceiving though, as position once on the green is critical and ultimately, it's the greens that provide the course with its defense against ridiculously low scores. Those greens and their secrets that are only revealed with repeated play are what allow well-past-their-prime former champions, and current Champions Tour members, Fred Couples and Bernhard Langer to consistently make cuts well into their 50s and, of course, it's why Jack Nicklaus was a threat to win here long after he stopped winning other events on the PGA Tour. Many forget that the Golden Bear had not one, not two, but three Top-10 finishes in the Masters *after* he won his celebrated sixth green jacket and 18th major in 1986.

Here are the Top 20 golfers in Strokes Gained, Putting at last year's Masters.

2018 Masters, Top SG:P Performers

Rank	Golfer	SG:P	Rounds
1	Kevin Kisner	8.82	4
2	Patrick Reed	8.56	4

3	Rickie Fowler	8.53	4
4	Paul Casey	6.10	4
5	Matt Kuchar	6.00	4
6	Tony Finau	5.60	4
7	Jose Maria Olazabal	5.14	2
8	Jon Rahm	4.59	4
9	Phil Mickelson	4.58	4
10	Daniel Berger	4.58	4
11	Matthew Fitzpatrick	4.29	4
12	Marc Leishman	4.05	4
13	Sandy Lyle	3.78	2
14	Jimmy Walker	3.14	4
15	Yuta Ikeda	3.12	2
15	Webb Simpson	3.05	4
17	Tommy Fleetwood	2.70	4
18	Bubba Watson	2.42	4
19	Jordan Spieth	2.41	4
20	Cameron Smith	2.25	4

What was it I just wrote about experience helping on the greens? Look at the putting display that two other former champions, Jose Maria Olazabal and Sandy Lyle put on in just two rounds. They may not have the power or precision in the other areas of their games to make the cut any more, but they can still putt with the best of today's pros on Augusta's greens.

Patrick Reed had to make up a little more than six strokes on the greens to beat Jordan Spieth by two strokes, and (see table, above) he did that, 8.56 Strokes Gained Putting to 2.41. Spieth, you can see, had a good tournament with the flat stick, finishing 19th in the field in Strokes Gained Putting, and 16th among those who made the cut. So what does it mean, tangibly, that Reed picked up six strokes putting versus Spieth?

One revealing piece of data is that Reed made 408 feet worth of putts over the course of the tournament compared to Spieth's 332 feet. Put another way, Reed had to overcome Spieth being closer to the hole thanks to superior driving and iron play by making more than an extra foot of putts on every hole over the course of the tournament.

There's an alternate way to look at this and it goes to repeatability. Reed outputted Spieth by roughly six Strokes Gained and 76 feet of made putts. There are an infinite number of ways that result can occur over 72 holes but, for simplicity, here's one way to express it. In a 15-foot putting contest, Reed made six more putts of that distance than Spieth, assuming Spieth left each of his misses about two feet away. That would mean Reed made roughly 80 more feet of putts than Spieth and, obviously, Reed would have six more Strokes Gained than Spieth.

I point all that out because it gets to the heart of the matter of handicapping the 2019 Masters. What do you think is more repeatable, Reed making six more 15-foot putts over 72 holes than another top-tier pro[13] or Spieth's elite play with irons in his hand?

One thing that the following five golfers hope is *not* repeatable is their performance on the putting greens at last year's Masters.

2018 Masters, Worst SG:P Performers

Rank	Golfer	SG:P	Rounds
87	Kyle Stanley	−9.34	4
86	Angel Cabrera	−7.05	2
85	Joaquin Niemann	−5.99	2
84	Yuxin Lin	−5.79	2
83	Bryson DeChambeau	−5.74	4

---

13. 15-foot putts are made roughly 22% of the time on the PGA Tour.

With the exception of former champion Cabrera, what really stands out here is the inexperience of the other four golfers who struggled mightily on the greens. Lin and Niemann were amateurs playing in their first Masters, DeChambeau was playing in the event for the first time as a pro, and Stanley's only other appearance in the event was a two-round showing, six years earlier in 2012. Without a doubt, DeChambeau is the most interesting name on the list as he's had a spectacular year on Tour since then and he was very good getting the ball to the green last year, ranking 22nd in Strokes Gained Tee to Green[14].

I have a million-dollar idea for any venue that hosts a PGA Tour event. Thanks to the laser precision of the ShotLink system, or in the case of the Masters, the Track system, it's possible to recreate any golf shot, within an inch of its original location, taken in a completed tournament. How much fun would it be to get a foursome and, starting the day after a tournament ends, go to all 18 greens and try to duplicate the putting success of the person who just won the tournament, or shot the best round, etc?

After a major, the demand for such an excursion would be overwhelming. The club overseeing the tournament would get to give their golf course a rest for say, an entire week while simply putting foursomes in golf carts and have them drive to each green where the location of each ball for the pro in question would be marked with a dot. They could charge $125 a person, $500 a foursome, and get the group of four around the course in two hours. After the Masters or the US Open, the host club could double that price and within a week, ta-da, it's a million-dollar idea.

If such an offer existed after the 2018 Masters, and if a group of

---

14. Strokes Gained Tee to Green calculations don't appear anywhere in this book but are simply the sum of Strokes Gained Off the Tee and Strokes Gained Approach and Around the Green. Or, alternatively, Total Strokes Gained minus Strokes Gained Putting.

amateurs decided they wanted to pit themselves against the greatest round of putting the tournament had seen that year, here's the challenge they would have faced.

First, picture you're in that foursome and you've spent a ton of time on the practice green at Augusta National, which by design is kept at the same speed as the 18 greens on the course. Are you feeling good? Is your stroke confident? Ok, because here is what you're going to have to do. It's not in the order you'll have to do it, but as you make your way to the first green, here's the task that you have ahead of you on what many pros assert are the toughest greens they encounter all year.

To complete this task as well as the pro you're imitating, you'll need to take only 23 putts today. Obviously, 18 of those putts are going to have to finish in the hole and they're going to average exactly 8 feet a putt, which of course is the distance at which pros make putts 50% of the time. Ok, here's what you have to do over 18 greens, starting from closest to the hole and moving back.

- You're going to face 18 first putts totaling 253 feet in length, with only four of them five feet or closer. Surprisingly, to match our pro, you get to two-putt one of those putts, a 3-footer on the 14th hole. That aside, you'll need to make the other three putts of five, four and two feet, respectively.

- Did you feel confident over that 5-footer you sunk? Good, because when we move to 6-footers on holes 2, 7, 11 and 13 you need to make them all.

- Now to 8 and 9 feet where the pro-conversion rate starts at 50% and drops rapidly as the distance increases. You need to make both of those putts.

- We'll next stop at 11 and 13 feet, and you'll need to drop both of those putts in too.

- At 15 feet, you get a reprieve, and just need to two-putt from that distance.

- Hopefully, you successfully converted that two-putt because you'll need to do it again, twice, from 24 feet.

- Have you digested all of that? *Now* it gets challenging. You'll need to drain putts from 26 and 35 feet before moving all the way back to 50 feet. Our pro two-putted from 50 feet so that's all you have to do, but for reference sake, let's note that he left his 50-foot putt a quarter-inch from the hole.

So that's it. If you make those 18 putts totaling 144 feet, you'll have matched the putting wizardry of Tony Finau during the first round of the 2018 Masters Tournament when he posted +4.91 SG. So much for the experience factor – like you and your foursome, that was Finau's first tournament round at Augusta. Oh, and if you really want to faithfully recreate his accomplishment, you need to do it less than 24 hours after self-administering to a dislocated ankle suffered while celebrating a hole-in-one on the Par 3 course[15].

---

15. If you haven't seen it, do yourself a favor and *don't* search for the video online.

Chapter 5

Augusta National,
Hole-by-Hole for Your Viewing Pleasure

So we've seen how each golfer performed at last year's tournament, but the charm of the Masters isn't just in watching the golfers who play the course, it's the course itself. What truly sets apart the Masters for viewers is familiarity with the venue, because as even casual golf fans know, this is the only major which is played on the same course every year. Even with familiarity however, viewers can still enhance the television experience with fresh data-driven insights. Using Strokes Gained data, viewing the Masters, already the most-watched golf telecast every single year, is even more compelling.

Before we begin our tour of Augusta National, here are a few final notes about the ways Strokes Gained are applied in a hole-by-hole context:

- The yardage for each hole is the base length of the hole according to Augusta National.

- The Strokes Gained Benchmark for each round is simply the average score on the hole during each round played in 2018. The overall average for the 2018 tournament is also listed to the right of the four daily average scores. (There were 280 rounds played in 2018, 87 each on Thursday and Friday and 53 on both Saturday and Sunday.)

- +/ − SG Tee Shot, Fairway Location is the benchmark ball location off the tee, and in the fairway, at which Strokes Gained Off the Tee toggles between negative and positive, based on last year's results. Closer to the green than the benchmark results in +SG and farther away means −SG. For balls off of the fairway that have an unobstructed shot to the green, 30 yards of extra distance is generally needed to overcome a ball in the rough vs. the fairway at a standard PGA Tour event. The rough, or "second cut" as it's known at Augusta, isn't as punishing as at many courses, so you can adjust that distance downward for golfers just off the fairways at Augusta. Tee shots in fairway bunkers or the woods will always result in −SG outcomes.

- +/ − SG Green Location after Approach is the benchmark, based on 2018 results, at which Strokes Gained after Approach (after tee shots on Par 3 holes, second shots on Par 4 holes, and third shots on Par 5 holes) toggles between positive and negative. Closer to the hole represents positive Strokes Gained to that point (i.e. +SG: Tee to Green) and farther away equates to negative Strokes Gained. Because Augusta has very little greenside rough or thick collars, balls off the green that are puttable have roughly the same Strokes Gained calculation as their same-distance-from-the-hole counterparts on the green.

- Strokes Gained Green Location after 2nd/3rd/4th shot lets you know how far a golfer's ball should be from the hole versus the Zero-Strokes-Gained benchmark after he's taken two, three or four shots on a par 3, 4 or 5 hole, respectively. (This will be after the first putt for holes on which the golfer hit the green in regulation.) Like the other benchmarks, closer to the pin than this distance represents +SG accrued so far and farther away is negative. Again, this is based on hole-specific data from the 2018 tournament.

Hole 1

Nickname: Tea Olive

Par: 4

Yards: 445

Strokes Gained Benchmark, by Round:	4.30[16]	4.34	4.30	4.11	4.28
+/- SG Tee Shot, Fairway Location:	188 yards from the flag				
+/- SG Green Location after Approach:	61 feet from the pin				
+/- SG Green Location after 3rd Shot:	5 feet from the hole				

Right out of the gate, Augusta National establishes its presence with authority (h/t Larry Biel) with this uphill, long par 4. The undulating green is particularly difficult to navigate as it took 510 putts over the 280 rounds played in 2018 for the golfers to complete the hole. That's an average of 1.82 putts per round, the highest of all 18 holes and is largely a testament to how hard it is to get approach shots close to the pin.

The overall difficulty didn't vary day-to-day with different pin placements, as the first green was one of only five which played tougher than the average PGA Tour green in all four rounds. Classifying all 18 greens over four rounds into 72-hole segments, Friday's pin placement on the left hand side of the green, guarded by the only greenside bunker on the hole and a false front short of the pin, resulted in this

---

16. One final note for those interested in Strokes Gained minutiae: In Chapter 3, I showed Jordan Spieth's Strokes Gained components for the first hole of the tournament, using 4.10 as the benchmark score. Since the hole actually played to 4.30 in round 1, therefore tougher than the average 445-yard hole on the PGA Tour, Spieth's Strokes Gained will be adjusted upwards to +0.30 from +0.10.

green playing the second toughest of any green on any day.

To make it even more challenging, thanks to a fairway bunker which attracted more than 10% of tee shots, this was also the toughest driving hole on the course over four days, and one of only three holes at Augusta tougher off the tee than an average driving hole on the PGA Tour. If your favorite golfer pars this hole he's picking up strokes on the field, and if he birdies it, as only 18 players did in 280 chances in 2018, his round is off to a tremendous start.

Hole 2

Nickname: Pink Dogwood

Par: 5

Yards: 575

Strokes Gained Benchmark, by Round: 4.90   4.84   4.74   4.68   4.81

+/- SG Tee Shot, Fairway Location: 294 yards from the flag

+/- SG Green Location after Approach: 13 feet from pin

+/- SG Green Location after 4th Shot: In hole

Despite being downhill, hole number two, the longest on the course, offers little respite after the difficulty of the opening hole. As is the case with just about every Par 5 on the PGA Tour, a score of par results in losing ground to the field, but it's not as pronounced on this hole because the green plays as the toughest on the course. In terms of visualizing the degree of difficulty, it equates to a 13-foot putt on this green getting made with the frequency of a 16-foot putt on the average PGA Tour green – a nearly 10% decrease in the standard PGA make rate.

Like hole number 1, the difficulty in sinking putts on this green did not vary a lot by pin location. Over the tournament's four rounds, ranking all 72 greens, the 2nd green finished 3rd, 12th, 32nd and 10th for each round, respectively, Thursday through Sunday.

Hole 3

Nickname: Flowering Peach
Par: 4
Yards: 350

Strokes Gained Benchmark, by Round:	4.07	3.76	3.96	3.94	3.93
+/- SG Tee Shot, Fairway Location:	118 yards from the flag				
+/- SG Green Location after Approach:	24 feet from pin				
+/- SG Green Location after 3rd Shot:	In hole				

This is the sole Par 4 on the course that some players attempt to drive. Only Tommy Fleetwood, in Round 2, pulled it off successfully last year, but those that pulled the driver out didn't seem to mind missing short and left, where many ultimate birdies still beckoned.

The hole played significantly easier on Friday, probably due to the back right pin location which gave the golfers more green to work with when holding a wedge in their hands. Although still tougher to putt than the average PGA Tour green, the 3rd green falls on the easier side of Augusta's 18 holes. Sunday's back left pin placement provided the best putting results for the field.

Hole 4

Nickname: Flowering Crab Apple
Par: 3
Yards: 240

Strokes Gained Benchmark, by Round:	3.36	3.44	3.26	3.11	3.32
+/- SG Tee Shot, Fairway Location:	N/A				
+/- SG Green Location after Tee Shot:	71 feet from pin				
+/- SG Green Location after 2nd Shot:	6 feet from the hole				

The length of the first Par 3 on the course makes the hole so challenging, a tee shot on the green but *still 71 feet from the hole* is the benchmark of success for anyone in the field.

This is the first hole on the course where pin placement made a huge difference in calculating green difficulty. Friday's pin placement in the back of the boomerang-shaped green gave the players all sorts of trouble and it ended up ranked the toughest of all 72 greens in the tournament. By contrast, on Thursday and Sunday it played easier than the average green on the PGA Tour.

Hole 5

Nickname: Magnolia
Par: 4
Yards: 455

Strokes Gained Benchmark, by Round:	4.25	4.18	4.11	4.04	4.16
+/- SG Tee Shot, Fairway Location:	196 yards from the flag				
+/- SG Green Location after Approach:	52 feet from pin				
+/- SG Green Location after 3rd Shot:	4 feet from the hole				

Overall, this hole plays the closest, in all aspects, to an average PGA hole as just small adjustments are needed to normalize the field's drives, approach shots and putts for difficulty. Like the hole that precedes it, the 5th hole's variation in difficulty from round to round is largely dependent on its pin placement. On Thursday it played as the 5th-toughest green (out of 72) of the tournament but on Sunday it was the 6th-easiest, by far the largest swing recorded by any green in 2018.

Even with the green putting "easy" though, it's still not a hole the field can collectively play under par due to the difficult tee shot. Hole 5 is one of only three holes, along with 1 and 17, that present the players with a more difficult drive than on the average PGA Tour tee box. The challenge here is similar to the challenge on the first tee; players must navigate an uphill dogleg hole (left in this case) with a pair of fairway bunkers waiting for anyone who is just a little imprecise or too aggressive with the angle of their drive.

Hole 6

Nickname: Juniper
Par: 3
Yards: 180

Strokes Gained Benchmark, by Round:	3.23	3.28	2.77	3.08	3.13
+/- SG Tee Shot, Fairway Location:	N/A				
+/- SG Green Location after Tee Shot:	45 feet from pin				
+/- SG Green Location after 2nd Shot:	4 feet from the hole				

Compared to Hole 4, the other Par 3 on the front side, the average entrant will be 26 feet closer to the pin after his tee shot. The green played progressively easier each round of the tournament so that by Sunday it had gone from a Top 10 hard putting hole to a Top 10 easy one.

Saturday's birdie bonanza was all about pin placement and accessibility from the tee. 53 golfers made 14 birdies on Saturday, four more than 174 golfers managed on Thursday and Friday combined. Even more telling was a near-total absence of bogeys. The third round featured just two bogeys, a rate of 3.8%. The bogey (or worse) rate for the other three days was 26%. So if you see the flag front and left this year, know that it is "go time" and anyone who doesn't walk off with a birdie will most likely lose ground to the field.

Hole 7

Nickname: Pampas
Par: 4
Yards: 450

Strokes Gained Benchmark, by Round:	4.39	4.36	3.91	3.96	4.21

+/- SG Tee Shot, Fairway Location: 186 yards from the flag
+/- SG Green Location after Approach: 53 feet from pin
+/- SG Green Location after 3rd Shot: 5 feet from the hole

It was a tale of two holes in 2018 – the one the full field played a third-of-a-stroke over par Thursday and Friday, and the one played under par on the weekend by those who made the cut. As we've seen on other holes, pin location and the resulting change in putting difficulty usually accounts for the difference in hole-specific, round-to-round scoring. That's not the case here, though, especially since both Thursday's *and* Sunday's green ranked among the top 10 hardest for all 72 holes. Instead, the roughly .40 stroke-per-golfer difference in pre – and post-cut scores may have had more to do with tee location as entrants had a much easier time getting tee shots in, and farther down the fairway the final two rounds. Through Friday, 43.7% of drives on the 7th hole found the fairway and all tee shots came to rest an average of 147 yards from the hole. In the final two rounds, the figures were 52.8% and 140 yards, respectively.

Hole 8

Nickname: Yellow Jasmine
Par: 5
Yards: 570

Strokes Gained Benchmark, by Round:	4.77	4.68	4.79	4.62	4.72
+/- SG Tee Shot, Fairway Location:	289 yards from the flag				
+/- SG Green Location after Approach:	12 feet from pin				
+/- SG Green Location after 4th Shot:	In the Hole				

Though it's a par 5 that plays under par every round of the tournament, the 8th hole does not surrender eagles easily. Reaching the hole in two is a challenge. The hole plays decidedly uphill and the fairway bunker snagged 17% of tee shots last year. Of the six eagles recorded here in 2018, only two were the result of a putt from the green.

Without the eagles, what keeps this hole reliably playing under par every single year, if not every round? An absence of greenside defenses compared to the three other par 5s. With a bunker-less green and no water in play, blow-ups are unlikely; last year the field recorded only one score worse than bogey in 280 attempts.

Hole 9

Nickname: Carolina Cherry
Par: 4
Yards: 460

Strokes Gained Benchmark, by Round:	4.16	4.32	4.02	3.94	4.14
+/- SG Tee Shot, Fairway Location:	183 yards from the flag				
+/- SG Green Location after Approach:	48 feet from pin				
+/- SG Green Location after 3rd Shot:	4 feet from the hole				

This is one of the easiest driving holes on the course, ranking just 11th in difficulty out of the 14 Par 4s and Par 5s and the easiest on the front side. With no fairway bunkers, and a fairly wide-open landing area, just 22 out of 280 tee shots wound up in a compromised position among trees, or sitting in pine straw. Interestingly, when the flag was placed closest to the famed "false front" on Sunday, the players posted their lowest scores, as that area of the green yielded the best putting results.

Hole 10

Nickname: Camellia

Par: 4

Yards: 495

Strokes Gained Benchmark, by Round:	4.13	4.25	4.00	3.81	4.08
+/- SG Tee Shot, Fairway Location:	195 yards from the flag				
+/- SG Green Location after Approach:	51 feet from pin				
+/- SG Green Location after 3rd Shot:	3 feet from the hole				

Like the front side of the course, the back begins with a stern test, in this case the listed #1 handicap hole on the course. In 2018, however, the players broke the cumulative scoring record in Masters play, averaging 4.082 strokes over the entire tournament, bettering the 4.121 mark that had stood since 1995.

The most obvious reason for the best-ever performance was the field's collective prowess on the green. The 10th green not only played the easiest, it was one of only three holes to grade out easier than the average PGA Tour green. There were a below-average 14 three-putts on the 10th green, but the real eye-opener was the distance of the average made putt. Across all 18 holes, the average length of a made putt at the 2018 Masters was 4.51 feet. At the 10th hole it was a tournament-high 5.39 feet. If the 10th green plays harder in 2019, scores will almost certainly return to their higher norm.

Hole 11

Nickname: White Dogwood

Par: 4

Yards: 505

Strokes Gained Benchmark, by Round:	4.36	4.56	4.28	4.32	4.40
+/- SG Tee Shot, Fairway Location:	226 yards from the flag				
+/- SG Green Location after Approach:	89 feet from pin				
+/- SG Green Location after 3rd Shot:	7 feet from the hole				

"Par is a good score here," is something you'll almost certainly hear while the CBS telecast features players on the 11th hole. And with very good reason. At last year's Masters, this hole was so difficult that in the final round, a score of par 4 on this hole was more valuable *than a birdie 4* on hole 13, as the field averaged 4.28 on the par 5 13th hole on Sunday compared to a 4.32 here.

Over the entire 2018 tournament, no one actually had a first putt greater than 89 feet, so essentially, any golfer that hits the green in regulation has achieved +SG Tee to Green.

Hole 12

Nickname: Golden Bell
Par: 3
Yards: 155

Strokes Gained Benchmark, by Round:	2.99	3.39	2.96	2.98	3.11
+/- SG Tee Shot, Fairway Location:	N/A				
+/- SG Green Location after Tee Shot:	49 feet from pin				
+/- SG Green Location after 2nd Shot:	4 feet from the hole				

If Augusta's 12th hole isn't ranked first among the most recognizable holes in golf, it's certainly on the composite scorecard. Given golf fans' familiarity with the shortest hole on the course, let's go into some detail to capture its difficulty.

Mark Broadie's exhaustive work tells us that holding all elements of a hole as average for the PGA Tour, professional Tour golfers will collectively play a 155-yard Par 3 to a score of 2.98 over time. The historic average score for all Masters Tournaments on the 12th hole is 3.28, and based on my research, the hole has never been altered. Here's what that means in terms of tee shot difficulty: For a par 3 with a 2.98 benchmark, a perfectly average tee shot would finish on the green, 30 feet from the hole. This would be perfectly average because those same Tour golfers would now have a 1.98 stroke benchmark to finish the hole. You can tell from above that last year a tee shot on the green 19 feet farther away than the Tour benchmark was average for the field – and Golden Bell played far easier last year than it traditionally has.

When the hole plays to its historic 3.28 average, any tee shot on the green inside 74 feet is above-average!

This hole's difficulty really is about a combination of three factors: the tee shot, which is subject to changing winds; a green shaped like a dining room table top; and Rae's Creek in front of the green. I have a friend who is a bigwig in Silicon Valley investing circles and has played Augusta a couple of times. After I crunched all the putting data, I asked him, "Once you're on the green, what's the easiest hole to putt on the course?" It took him no more than five seconds to answer, "the 12th." The data, from last year at least, supports that. The 12th green was one of only three that played easier than the average PGA Tour green and was the second-easiest overall. Getting the ball on the green of this architectural gem is the tough part, but once you're there, the green plays like a pool table.

Hole 13

Nickname: Azalea

Par: 5

Yards: 510

Strokes Gained Benchmark, by Round:	4.64	4.77	4.64	4.28	4.61
+/- SG Tee Shot, Fairway Location:	236 yards from the flag				
+/- SG Green Location after Approach:	10 feet from pin				
+/- SG Green Location after 4th Shot:	In the hole				

Augusta National is so associated with the flower for which the 13th hole is named that Sergio Garcia and his wife bestowed the name upon their first-born daughter, shortly after he won the 2017 tournament, his first major championship[17]. Of course, the 13th hole, the final of the famed Amen Corner trio, is also one of the most pivotal holes on the course. Barely longer than the Par 4 11th hole, par is *not* a good score on this hole. The hole played so easy last year, especially in the 4th round where the field averaged 4.28, that there were nearly as many eagles on the weekend (5) as bogeys or worse (6).

What makes this hole special, and as mentioned above, "pivotal," is the dispersion around the second shot for those who have executed a tee shot well enough to bring the green into play for their second shot. Because a well-struck iron makes eagle a distinct possibility, while a less-than-perfect shot brings the chance of a bogey, there's huge leverage on the second shot. The distinct possibility of poor

---

17. As the father to a Lily, I say, well done Garcia family, well done.

results made the 13th hole the 2nd-most difficult approach shot on the course in 2018, and the most difficult, the approach on the 15th hole, had its results skewed by Garcia's six-approach-shot score of 13.

Hole 14

Nickname: Chinese Fir

Par: 4

Yards: 440

Strokes Gained Benchmark, by Round:	4.30	4.07	3.83	3.87	4.06
+/- SG Tee Shot, Fairway Location:	173 yards from the flag				
+/- SG Green Location after Approach:	36 feet from pin				
+/- SG Green Location after 3rd Shot:	3 feet from the hole				

With just a mild dogleg-left shaping, and no bunkers (the only hole on the course without one) the 14th hole is left only with a sloping, tiered green to defend itself against an onslaught of birdies. In 2018 that was enough. The 14th green played the second-toughest on the back side, and was especially difficult in the first two rounds, when the pins were farther from the back of the green and closer to the false front.

The putting statistics were broadly representative of how the Augusta's greens as a whole played over the entire tournament. That is, tough on Thursday and Friday and quite a bit easier Saturday and (especially) Sunday. Yes, the weekend field consists of better golfers who survived the cut, but a more forgiving setup appears to be at play as well.

Hole 15

Nickname: Firethorn

Par: 5

Yards: 530

Strokes Gained Benchmark, by Round:	4.64	4.86	4.43	4.66	4.68
+/- SG Tee Shot, Fairway Location:	235 yards from the flag				
+/- SG Green Location after Approach:	11 feet from pin				
+/- SG Green Location after 4th Shot:	In the hole				

Like its Par 5 counterpart two holes earlier, the 15th also features the opportunity to attempt a high-leverage second shot over water to set up an eagle putt. Scores aren't quite as low here as they are on 13 but a score of par still drops a meaningful margin to the field.

Patrick Reed won the "Par 5 tournament[18]" last year en route to his green jacket and he did most of his damage on 13 and 15. He shot − 13 on the par 5s, and his work on 15 really stood out, and probably paved the way to victory. Reed needed just 3 putts on the 15th green all tournament, sinking putts of seven and six feet for birdies on Thursday and Friday and then chipping in from 27 yards away on Saturday for an eagle resulting in a five-shot lead which he needed every bit of over the final 21 holes of the tournament to secure his first major championship.

---

18. Louis Oosthuizen won the "Par 3 tournament" with a score of − 4 over the 16 par 3 holes. Jordan Spieth finished second at − 3 while Patrick Reed shot an abysmal +4. Although it happens far less than many might suspect, last year's champion owed his success to his performance on the Par 5s, while being weighed down by his Par 3 results.

Hole 16

Nickname: Redbud

Par: 3

Yards: 170

Strokes Gained Benchmark, by Round:	2.97	3.16	3.04	2.91	3.03
+/- SG Tee Shot, Fairway Location:	N/A				
+/- SG Green Location after Tee Shot:	29 feet from pin				
+/- SG Green Location after 2nd Shot:	2 feet from the hole				

The 12th hole might be the most recognizable at Augusta, but if you walked any true fan of the Masters out to the 16th green and told them to put dots on the ground for the pin placement during Saturday's and Sunday's round, they wouldn't need Google Maps to come within inches of the exact location. I can't prove it, but I strongly suspect I first learned the phrase "traditional Sunday pin placement" from Verne Lundquist discussing this very hole.

The 16th really is a tale of two holes, for when the pin is atop the right-side hill as it almost always is during the third round, it's a difficult green to putt, last year ranking as the toughest green prior to Sunday. But when the pin is back and left, free of the tiers to the right, the players can take aim at a flat putting surface and past Sunday feats of David Love III, Jack Nicklaus and, of course, Tiger Woods are recalled every year.

On the other hand, the only two four-putts of the entire 2018 tournament both happened on this green. Angel Cabrera (round 2) and Justin Thomas (round 4) are hoping their "feats" won't be recalled, or at least repeated, in future years.

Hole 17

Nickname: Nandina
Par: 4
Yards: 440

Strokes Gained Benchmark, by Round:	4.14	4.26	4.11	4.13	4.17
+/- SG Tee Shot, Fairway Location:	185 yards from the flag				
+/- SG Green Location after Approach:	53 feet from pin				
+/- SG Green Location after 3rd Shot:	4 feet from the hole				

Possibly best known as the former location of the Eisenhower tree (a 2014 ice storm finally removed the 34th president's nemesis more than 50 years after his futile request), the 17th hole nonetheless has a distinctive feature that keeps the average score above par. Thanks to playing straight uphill, this ends up being the second-hardest driving hole on the course after the first hole, and along with the 5th, one of only three harder than the average Tour drive.

The toggle point for a + or − SG:OTT designation on 17, 185 yards from the flag and in the fairway, provides a tangible data point for comparison with number 14 which is exactly the same length. On 14, the 'break-even' distance, if you will, for a quality drive in the fairway is 12 yards closer to the hole.

Hole 18

Nickname: Holly

Par: 4

Yards: 465

Strokes Gained Benchmark, by Round:	4.21	4.03	4.09	4.04	4.10
+/- SG Tee Shot, Fairway Location:	201 yards from the flag				
+/- SG Green Location after Approach:	42 feet from pin				
+/- SG Green Location after 3rd Shot:	4 feet from the hole				

The players must tackle a second straight uphill hole to finish their round. It may be 25 yards longer than the 17th, and includes a fairway bunker to snag tee shots, but an "average" drive in the fairway is only 16 yards farther away from the flag than on 17. Not only that but approach shots on 18, must be 11 feet closer to the hole so as not to drop strokes to the field tee-to-green. That's because the uphill slope of the 18th hole isn't nearly as steep as 17's.

Getting the ball on the green after the drive on the 18th hole graded out as the easiest on the course last year, suggesting the two bunkers surrounding the green don't cause the pros much trouble. That calculation was aided by nine (!) different hole-outs from off the green. Considering there were only 28 hole-outs the entire tournament[19], that's an astounding figure. Excluding the hole-outs, the field still did well getting on the green. The average length of a player's first

---

19. The official tournament statistics are almost certainly higher because, when supported by video or graphic evidence, I treated balls putted from barely off the green on Augusta's perfectly manicured collars as putts for Strokes Gained classification rather than scrambles from around the green.

putt on the 18th green over the course of the tournament was 17.0 feet, lowest of any par 4 on the back side and third-lowest overall which includes the nearly-drivable 3rd hole.

CHAPTER 6

A 2019 Masters Preview

When it comes to projecting a golfer's performance, there are two great debates within the fantasy golf and golf betting communities: How much weight to put on course history and how much weight to put on a golfer's recent form versus his historic results? There is no fully-embraced or "correct" answer for either question, and I'm not even going to suggest the proper formula as it depends on a lot of different inputs a gamer or handicapper might use. Of course, deciding which factors to use and how heavily to depend on them is the alluring part of the entire exercise. Or, as the late Tom Petty might say, the weighting is the hardest part.

Let's look at course history first. There may not be a "correct" answer, but I can tell you there are a number of oft-repeated phrases in fantasy and betting circles that have little value. They include, "Golfer X is seven for nine in cuts made at this event and has four top-20 finishes including two top-10s." or "A winner here in 2014, so-and-so golfer is always comfortable in his home state." If there's anything I'd like readers to take away from this book, it's to largely ignore any analysis that isn't Strokes Gained-based.

So let's use Strokes Gained to look at the puzzle that is course history and see how much to rely on the "horses for courses" factor when projecting Masters results. Most examinations of this topic focus on the golfers, but when first examined from the standpoint of the course, in the case of Augusta National, it provides a striking revelation.

To reiterate, I don't care about final position on the leaderboard, cuts made, money won, etc.; to evaluate the predictive nature of a player's past results at a tournament, I will solely rely on Strokes Gained history. My PGA Tour data set dates back to 1996, the year Tiger Woods turned pro. I took the Strokes Gained results for every player that played in the Masters in the last 23 years (1996-2018) and, if they played the following year, calculated the correlation between their Strokes Gained in year T and year T+1.

First, some context. I've done this calculation for every PGA event and on average the calculation yields a year-to-year correlation in Strokes Gained of .16 and anything above .20 is considered high, even if you're in the camp who might not consider that *strong* correlation. **For the Masters that same calculation yields a correlation of .40.** There is no other tournament that comes anywhere close to that figure, with the Bay Hill Invitational the second-highest at .23. And there's not a ton of variation either, based on the time frame you select. The Masters correlation over just the last five years is .37.

So, you might be thinking, maybe there's a reason for that high figure relating to the golfers in the tournament. After all, the Masters consists of an elite field of golfers and since the other majors, with somewhat bigger fields, are played on different courses each year, there's no other tournament to reliably compare it to.

I'd counter that The Players Championship contested each year at TPC Sawgrass should provide a meaningful comparison. While the field at The Players is larger, and therefore not quite as elite, the bottom quarter of the Tour turns over each year so the same golfers that play in one year and then the next, will be quite similar to the

Masters. Further, if you're looking for similar-sized, invitation-only fields that attract elite golfers, The Memorial, Arnold Palmer Invitational at Bay Hill and the WGC/Bridgestone event at Akron provide good comparisons. Here are the average yearly correlations for those four tournaments, also held 1996-2018.

	'96-'18	'13-'18
The Players	.16	.05
WGC, Akron[20]	.22	.19
Bay Hill	.23	.26
The Memorial	.18	.11
The Masters	.40	.37

As you can see, individual golfer's year-over-year performance on other courses doesn't come anywhere close to exhibiting the persistence it does at Augusta. That's the course side of the equation and in the case of the Masters it confirms we should take a look at the players to determine their course factor. Here again, I'm going to differ with a lot of what you may have read on this topic. To my mind, it doesn't matter how well or how poorly a golfer has played on a particular course over time if it's absent context. What I care about is how well a golfer performed in a tournament *compared to his then-current form*, which I'm going to define as how well he played over the entire season[21]. That way, like the Strokes Gained calculation, it's a zero-sum calculation for each golfer across all his tournaments he played that year. For an example of the calculation,

---

20. The 2002 event was held in Sahalee, Washington so 2001-2002 and 2002-2003 correlations are omitted.

21. You can make the case that the best measure of current form against which to compare a golfer's results at a single tournament would be to compare how he performed over a symmetrical amount of events on either side of the tournament. I have no trouble with the logic of that argument. For simplicity though, and because I believe golfers need baseball-like statistics as presented by FanGraphs or Baseball-Reference, I think of everything in terms of stand-alone seasons.

let's take a look at the lifetime work of Bubba Watson at the Masters.

I guarantee you that if you search the internet for articles and blogs dispensing fantasy or betting advice for the Masters, Bubba Watson's name will appear favorably. And why not? You'll surely see his name alongside factual phrases such as "two-time winner" and "made 9 of 10 career cuts at Augusta" and "three Top-10 finishes" and maybe even commentary that includes wording similar to this: "he's the ultimate example of a 'horses for courses' pro."

Let's put that thinking under the data-centric, Strokes Gained microscope for context. Bubba Watson has played 38 rounds of golf in the Masters, as reflected in the "9 of 10 cuts" statement above. In those 38 rounds, he's accrued 42.65 Strokes Gained. That's an average of 1.12 Strokes Gained per round. In those same ten seasons, Watson averaged 0.93 Strokes Gained per round. Yes, that's a positive Course Factor of 0.19 Strokes Gained per round, but I suspect it's much smaller than any golf fan would guess. Here's another way to look at it that may surprise you. Watson has amassed 7.22 more Strokes Gained in his ten Masters appearances than you'd expect if he'd performed exactly the same at the Masters as he had the rest of that same season. Last year, with 11.11 Strokes Gained for the Tournament against his entire 2018 performance of 0.58 Strokes Gained per round, Watson accrued 8.78 (11.11 − (4★ 0.58) more Strokes Gained than his baseline performance for the year. So that means, prior to 2018, Watson, a two-time winner of the event in nine tries actually *had a negative course* factor for the Masters. I'm positive you wouldn't have read or heard that anywhere prior to the start of last year's tournament.

To help determine if there are any other narrative-busting conclusions in the data, below are the Course Factor calculations for any 2019 Masters invitee as of 12/31/18, excluding Senior Tour players, who has played a minimum of 20 rounds at Augusta.

Golfer	Entries	Rounds	Career SG	SG/ Rd	+/ – SG vs. Exp.	Course Factor
Jordan Spieth	5	20	65.19	3.26	31.71	+1.59 SG/Rd
Phil Mickelson	23	86	195.9	2.28	72.65	0.84
Charley Hoffman	5	20	26.15	1.31	15.41	0.77
Hideki Matsuyama	7	26	30.31	1.17	12.96	0.50
Justin Rose	13	52	92.46	1.78	25.16	0.48
Paul Casey	12	42	49.82	1.19	17.62	0.42
Jimmy Walker	5	20	19.19	0.96	6.11	0.31
Tiger Woods	20	78	205.17	2.63	23.4	0.30
Rickie Fowler	8	30	40.95	1.36	5.93	0.20
Bubba Watson	10	38	42.65	1.12	7.22	0.19
Matt Kuchar	12	46	53.36	1.16	8.61	0.19
Brandt Snedeker	10	36	32.88	0.91	6.69	0.19
Jason Day	8	29	47.14	1.63	2.60	0.09
Adam Scott	17	64	74.7	1.17	4.34	0.07
Louis Oosthuizen	10	32	24.04	0.75	0.39	0.01
Charl Schwartzel	9	30	24.72	0.82	-1.32	-0.04
Rory McIlroy	10	38	58.71	1.54	-1.74	-0.05
Stewart Cink	17	58	47.14	0.81	-4.16	-0.07
Dustin Johnson	8	30	34.92	1.16	-7.83	-0.26
Zach Johnson	14	44	18.96	0.43	-21.67	-0.49
Sergio Garcia	20	68	41.51	0.61	-36.51	-0.54
Charles Howell III	8	26	5.03	0.19	-14.83	-0.57
Henrik Stenson	13	44	20.93	0.48	-25.38	-0.58
Martin Kaymer	11	34	-8.15	-0.24	-20.78	-0.61
Kevin Na	7	22	-3.41	-0.15	-16.16	-0.73
Webb Simpson	7	22	4.04	0.18	-17.41	-0.79
Francesco Molinari	7	24	-0.24	-0.01	-21.26	-0.89

Your preconceived narratives may differ from mine or those that you'll hear leading up to the tournament, but here are a couple of takeaways that surprised me:

- Jordan Spieth's 5-year record at Augusta is astoundingly good. Tiger Woods' best 5-year Strokes Gained stretch of 69.89 edges Spieth's 65.19, but otherwise there is no modern equivalent. Interestingly, Tiger's best stretch was also across his first five Masters as a pro, 1997-2001.

- Phil Mickelson has raised his game at Augusta like no other player over as long a time frame. A +0.84 per round Course Factor on top of his already elevated standard of excellence for 20+ years is truly impressive.

- Rory McIlroy, with more than 58 Strokes Gained over just 38 rounds (+1.54 SG round) has certainly played well at Augusta, but no better than he normally plays, and that's what the Course Factor calculation captures.

- Dustin Johnson hasn't played any better than Matt Kuchar at Augusta, as both have averaged 1.16 SG per round over their careers. That's notable, of course, because over their similar-length careers, DJ is the far better golfer. You would think Johnson's skills would be well-suited to Augusta – again that's reflected in the narrative and often the betting line – but the results-to-date don't show it.

So that's the Course Factor calculation, but what about the baseline performance it's used to adjust?

You could go to the Statistics section of PGATour.com and find the Strokes Gained data for 2019 but that will just have results since last October, starting with the Safeway Classic. You could use the 2018 season data, but there's no way to merge the two years. In any event, as I've alluded to elsewhere in this book, there are shortcomings in the PGA's Strokes Gained data, namely it doesn't include any events that lack ShotLink readings. Additionally, the data is unadjusted for strength-of-fields faced.

Baseball has WAR,[22] football YAR[23] and basketball has Win Shares and PER,[24] measurement standards which attempt to standardize player performance in a context-neutral setting. In other words raw performance figures are normalized for playing time, strength of opponent, park factors, etc. and converted to a single figure against which all other players can be measured. Golf, as all recreational amateurs are aware, has a handicap system that attempts to accomplish the same goal. But when it comes to ranking golfers at the professional level, the basis for comparison is typically money won, or Fed Ex points earned or the Official World Ranking, all of which vastly overstate the value of winning a tournament in terms of ranking players solely by their exhibited skills. To overcome those shortcomings, what follows is a listing of all eligible full-time PGA Tour event golfers who have qualified for this year's Masters (as of 12/31/18) sorted by a metric which includes total Strokes Gained for every PGA Tour event, adjusted for strength-of-fields faced. It is scaled to zero, the average PGA Touring Pro, as I described Scott Piercy in Chapter 1. I call the metric PAR, or Performance vs. Average per Round. This isn't just a theoretical calculation from my perspective. It's the starting point, prior to tweaks for Course Factors, recent performance adjustments, or the effect of a golfer's aging curve on his future performance, for all of my head-to-head betting calculations. Here is the PAR ranking of relevant entrants of this year's Masters based on their results from the 2017-2018 season and 2018-2019 season through 12/31/18:

---

22. Wins Above Replacement player

23. Yards Above Replacement player

24. Player Efficiency Rating

PAR of 2019 Masters Participants as of 12/31/18
(minimum 40 rounds played)

Golfer	PAR
Dustin Johnson	2.35
Justin Rose	2.05
Justin Thomas	1.83
Tony Finau	1.61
Jason Day	1.61
Rickie Fowler	1.60
Tommy Fleetwood	1.57
Bryson DeChambeau	1.48
Webb Simpson	1.43
Brooks Koepka	1.42
Tiger Woods	1.40
Patrick Cantlay	1.32
Paul Casey	1.24
Rory McIlroy	1.19
Rafa Cabrera Bello	1.18
Patrick Reed	1.17
Hideki Matsuyama	1.14
Jon Rahm	1.13
Henrik Stenson	1.03
Francesco Molinari	1.03
Phil Mickelson	0.98
Marc Leishman	0.98
Emiliano Grillo	0.97
Alex Noren	0.97
Gary Woodland	0.97
Jordan Spieth	0.96
Zach Johnson	0.92
Keegan Bradley	0.84
Tyrell Hatton	0.79
Billy Horschel	0.75

Adam Scott	0.75
Matt Kuchar	0.75
Charles Howell III	0.73
Kyle Stanley	0.72
Louis Oosthuizen	0.67
Aaron Wise	0.67
Xander Schauffele	0.64
Branden Grace	0.62
Ian Poulter	0.60
Cameron Smith	0.60
Bubba Watson	0.58
Kevin Na	0.50
Kiradech Aphibarnrat	0.41
Charley Hoffman	0.35
Brandt Snedeker	0.33
Stewart Cink	0.29
Matthew Fitzpatrick	0.23
Kevin Kisner	0.22
Kevin Tway	0.21
Jimmy Walker	0.15
Si Woo Kim	0.13
Patton Kizzire	0.01
Hao Tong Li	-0.09
Charl Schwartzel	-0.26
Andrew Landry	-0.27
Satoshi Kodaira	-0.82
Michael Kim	-1.18

As a reminder, here's a summary of what the table represents: Each entrant's PAR is how much you'd expect him to beat the average Touring Pro in a round of golf if both played at exactly the same performance level they demonstrated over the last year or so. In the case of the Masters' field, Patton Kizzire is the average Touring Pro.

So, with last year's Masters Strokes Gained report, the historic course factor for those with at least 20 rounds of experience, and performance over the last year, golf fans are armed with data about what happened in the past. But what does it mean for the future?

I'll take a shot at that.

Here's my predicted finish for the 2019 Masters as of publication on Tuesday, February 5, 2019. It takes into account all of the above information, as well as PGA Tour performance during the first five tournaments of calendar year 2019.

Joe Peta's Predicted
Top 10 Order of Finish, 2019 Masters

10. **Jordan Spieth**. There is a lot to dislike about his current arc of performance. The putting woes get a lot of attention but that doesn't account for all of the steep drop-off in play. The PAR rankings for 2015 and 2017 would have had Spieth's name at the top so it's a bit shocking, *at age 25*, to see him sharing company with Alex Noren, Emiliano Grillo and Gary Woodland in this year's rankings. Remember, the Course Factor calculations measure how well a golfer performed at Augusta versus his current form at the time, and Spieth's current form has never been lower entering the Masters than it is this year. Still, his previous success at Augusta can't be ignored and it's enough to project a Top-10 finish, which would be his fifth in six appearances.

9. **Brooks Koepka**. There's no detailed Strokes Gained data for Koepka in the prior pages at the Masters because he missed last year's tournament with an injured wrist. Still he's made three cuts here in three tries and amassed nearly +13 SG over those 12 rounds. He's also played consistently well posting positive SG rounds in 75% of his rounds. Factor in strength-of-field and Koepka's played to roughly his baseline level every year at Augusta. Of course, his baseline level of performance has never been higher having won three events, including two majors in the last year.

8. **Dustin Johnson.** There's a lot to suggest that although it didn't feature a major championship, 2018 marked the peak of Johnson's career in terms of consistency of elite performance. Unless you are Tiger Woods[25], a year with Adjusted[26] Strokes Gained per Round above 2.5 isn't repeated[27]. In addition to that regression, at nearly 35 he's at the apex of a professional golfer's aging curve and his overall Masters resume isn't sparkling. Still, his core skills are so good and his tee-bombing, birdie-centric game so suited for Augusta, even a slight slippage in baseline performance this year makes him a threat to win it all.

7. **Rickie Fowler.** Honestly, all the talk about where Fowler fits in the "best golfers never to have won a major" discussion is a bit overdone in my eyes. For as much attention as he gets, Fowler's round-by-round body of work from 2010-2016 – 529 Strokes Gained over 570 rounds – is reminiscent of a PGA Tour grinder. Flirting with +1 SG a round for years is Bill Hass-like and no one is including him in conversations featuring Colin Montgomerie, Lee Westwood or Steve Stricker. To be fair, Fowler truly had a breakout year in 2017 (+1.97 SG per round) – taking what Bill Simmons would call "the leap" – and he didn't suffer too much regression in 2018 (+1.53 SG per round.) Having just turned 30, a peak age for year-over-year SG advances, with a good Course Factor and demonstrated excellence with the irons and the putter in last year's event, Fowler is a true contender. But if he does win, let's go easy with the "monkey off his back" idiom. This isn't John Elway winning a Super Bowl.

6. **Bryson DeChambeau.** In his first appearance at Augusta as a pro last year, DeChambeau slayed the course off the tee, maintained

---

25. See Table in Chapter 1 and then chuckle at the idea today's Tour elites are at Tiger's peak level.

26. Adjusted for strength-of-fields faced. For 2018, DJ's Raw SG per round was 2.403 and his Adj SG per round was 2.712.

27. Vijay Singh, in 2003 and 2004, is the only other person of this era to do it.

that better-than-the-field pace getting to the greens and then gave it all back putting. While experience and a heady approach should help one year later, putting weakness is the wrong area of vulnerability to have at Augusta. That's the only thing that keeps DeChambeau, riding a favorable aging curve and a rising arc of performance that includes four Tour victories since last year's Masters, from a Top 5 projection.

5. **Hideki Matsuyama.** I don't believe sushi has ever been served at the annual Champions Dinner but that sure would be a nice change of pace, wouldn't it? Matsuyama has a terrific history of performance at the Masters with 10 of his last 16 rounds gaining at least two strokes on the field. Perhaps because of those years of excellence and his five PGA Tour victories, I'm always surprised when I'm reminded he'll be just 27 at this year's tournament. His PAR ranking dipped in 2018, but that was unquestionably impacted by a thumb injury which limited his play and his success. Even so, he still managed to record his sixth-straight season averaging more than +1 SG per round.

4. **Justin Rose.** You can make some of the same caveats about Rose's outlook in 2019 that you can about Dustin Johnson's, adding that Rose is 38 years old. However, while there are signs in the round-by-round data suggesting Johnson's slide from his peak has already started, that's not the case with Rose. Given Rose isn't considered a true bomber in the Rory/DJ/Koepka class and that he's carried the stigma of being weak with the flat stick in his career, you might be surprised to see just how fantastic and consistent he's been over 52 rounds at Augusta. I don't think it's unfair to call this his last, best chance to win the Masters, but it's still a very realistic one in 2019 for a golfer who is not just at the top of his game, but atop everyone else's game as well.

3. **Tiger Woods.** Although it may have taken his victory at last year's Tour Championship to definitively answer the question, "Is Tiger back?" it probably shouldn't have. Take a deep look at performance aging curves of PGA Tour golfers and apply them to Tiger Woods

and you'd find that +1.57 SG per round, as Tiger posted in 2018, would be roughly what you'd expect for a 42-year old golfer who posted +3 SG per round while he was in his 20s. Tiger was back before the goosebump-inducing walk to the 18th green at East Lake and if you didn't think so, you need to realize the age-20 Mike Trout who stole 49 bases is never coming back either. I use, roughly, a golfer's last 40 rounds, which is about half a season, but however you want to define "current form," in Tiger's case it's even better than his overall 2018 results. His Course Factor at the Masters is hampered a bit by the unreal baseline he has to overcome and he has still improved on that over his career. Here's an astounding fact for Tiger at Augusta: In his 76 rounds at the Masters as a pro, he's only had ten negative SG rounds. That 87% success rate is unparalleled over that time period, minimum 30 rounds played[28]. Two of those ten rounds happened last year, when, as mentioned, he hadn't truly found his 2018 form yet. I don't think anyone would mind if this call ends up being too conservative.

2. **Jon Rahm.** Because he's only played in two Masters, totaling 8 rounds, Rahm didn't appear in the Course Factor rankings, but if he did it would have been in fourth place. Looking at his Strokes Gained components last year, you have to love the displayed excellence in all areas of his game. His booming drives should have him in contention here every year and at just 23, every aspect of his game should still be on the rise. His 2018 results may not overwhelm you, but Rahm had the second-highest strength-of-field adjustment on the PGA Tour last year, behind only Tommy Fleetwood, meaning the two Europeans played the toughest slate of events of anyone on Tour in 2018.

1. **Tony Finau.** Talk about taking "the leap." Finau, despite being only 28-years-old at the time, entered 2018 as a "journeyman,"

---

28. Phil Mickelson comes closest at 65 out of 82 rounds (79%). Jordan Spieth, at 85% after 20 rounds played needs to actually better his excellence over three more tournaments to exceed Tiger's rate.

having turned professional more than a decade earlier while still a teenager. He plied his craft worldwide until getting to the PGA Tour in 2015 and "securing" future membership for two years with a 2016 win in an unheralded event in Puerto Rico. With the security of a Tour card in hand, he crossed over the +1 SG per round threshold in 2017, but was still a Tour afterthought entering 2018. That's no longer the case.

Last year, Finau turned into a birdie machine (2nd in total birdies) en route to eleven Top-10 finishes and a #4 spot in the 2018 PAR rankings. As the last pick on the 2018 Ryder Cup team he wound up being a rare American bright spot, punctuated with a singles match thrashing of EU golden boy, Tommy Fleetwood. Then he opened 2019 with a playoff loss at the WGC-HSBC Champions event, his fourth second-place finish in just over a season.

Still, because his round-by-round excellence didn't feature a Tour victory, he gets dismissed when conversations turn to the elite contenders. This stat should squash that sentiment: Since last year's U.S. Open, my starting point for current form, Finau has an ultra-elite Adjusted Strokes Gained per round of 2.21 over 52 rounds. During that same time period only Dustin Johnson at 2.28 per round and Justin Rose at 2.69 are better. But Finau's figures are compiled over 73% more rounds than Rose and 37% more than Johnson. Fifty-plus rounds, adjusted for field strength, above 2.2 SG per round is knocking on the door of "best in the world." But Finau is only 29 and my work with aging curves suggests the biggest leap in year-over-year performance happens somewhere right around the Age-29/Age-30 season.

I find David Duval's struggle two decades ago to break through with a Tour win similar to Finau's plight. Like Finau today, Duval was Top-20 ranked golfer in 1997 known in cynical circles for his failure to win a tournament. When the victory finally came at the now-defunct Michelob Championship, it unleashed a torrent of victories – an incredible 11 over the next 18 months. Finau's level of play suggests there could be a winning streak in his future and there would be no better place to start it than the grounds of Augusta National.

Chapter 7

Wanna Bet? A Brief
Primer on Golf Betting

W idely regarded by serious sports bettors as the best sportsbook in the world, Pinnacle enjoys a sterling reputation for its customer-friendly approach to the business of bookmaking and its "winners welcome" policy. I'm still listed as one of their featured authors in their website's Betting Resources section, dating back to when I wrote some articles and held an Ask Me Anything session for the site. So you certainly won't be surprised to know that I hold Pinnacle in the same high regard as the rest of the sports-betting universe.

With one exception. When it comes to golf futures for winning a PGA tournament, Pinnacle is no better than a shady Costa Rican online sportsbook/casino and it drives me nuts[29].

Golf futures are just as unbettable at Pinnacle as they are everywhere else, including the best of Las Vegas' physical sportsbooks. The simple

---

29. As an American, I am unable to open an account with Pinnacle, so the frustration lies in observing the divergent business practice of an industry leader, combined with my experience as a Wall Street market maker in much larger markets where I was certainly at a bigger informational disadvantage than any bookmaker would find itself dealing golf futures.

way to reach that conclusion for yourself is to convert the listed odds for each golfer into an implied win percentage and then sum the total. Of course, you don't have to (and you shouldn't) limit this calculation to golf futures. You can take the standard – 110 line for any football or basketball game and realize that when you have the option to bet $110 to win $100 on either team in a game, each team is being assigned a 52.38% win probability (110 / (110 + 100)). From a business perspective, the best way to think of this is that the bookmaker is selling a $100 bill in two pieces that add up to $104.76 (2 * 52.38) which is a fair gross margin for a bookmaker to extract from its customers[30].

Now take a look at that calculation when it comes to betting on a single golfer to win a tournament. Regardless of the tournament, all sportsbooks, including Pinnacle, the Westgate and South Point, to name three of the very best sportsbooks overseas and in Vegas, sell that $100 bill in pieces that add up to at least $130 and often $140. That means there is zero chance that placing a bet on a golfer to win a tournament has a positive expected value. That *has* to be your default assumption. And I say that having a few pages earlier described a golfer I think has demonstrated "best in the world" skills yet is currently listed with better odds than ten or so other golfers in the field. Even placing a bet on him carries no other value than receiving the surge of excitement and eventual emotional satisfaction that comes from solving a puzzle correctly if he wins. It's paying for fun, in the same sense as buying a video game or going to a movie.

So what's a sports bettor to do? Well, while futures betting has entertainment value, the money is in the matchups.

---

30. Baseball betting, which features moneyline betting as opposed to pointspread betting uses a "dime line" convention so that the default – 105/-105 bet equates to selling that same $100 bill for just $102.44, a huge advantage versus $104.76 in football betting. But wait, it gets better! That's the *worst* margin you'll ever face as a baseball bettor, and it only exists for a game between two evenly matched teams. As detailed in my book *Trading Bases*, the average hurdle a serious baseball bettor faces over the course of a year is navigating pieces of a $100 bill that add up to a hair under $102. Baseball betting is great.

Before each tournament and before each round, sportsbooks will offer head-to-head betting between two golfers and the price, or house margin, will be identical to betting on a football or basketball game. In other words, if you're armed with good data, it's an endeavor where you at least have a chance to achieve a positive return over time.

We don't know the matchups that will be offered for the 2019 Masters yet, but regardless of how the golfers are paired up, the math behind any potential play is the same. Whether you use my PAR calculations as a starting point, apply any number of possible factor adjustments or completely build your own model from scratch, you're trying to determine how much better one golfer is than another per round of golf played. Once you do that, you can convert that margin into an expected win percentage. For those of you not inclined to build your own simulator, here's a cheat sheet[31]:

Heads-Up Expected Win Percentages, Over Four Rounds

Golfer	Stroke per Round Edge	Expected Win %[32]
A	.25	56%
B		44%
A	.50	61%
B		39%
A	.75	65%
B		35%
A	1.00	70%
B		30%

It's rare for the books to pair up golfers with a huge disparity in

---

31. Datagolf.ca has a very helpful simulator under its interactive tools section.

32. Expected Win % factors out ties as those are graded as "pushes" or no action, and all bets are returned. So if a simulation returns win expectancies for golfers A and B as 50% and 45%, respectively, with a 5% chance of a tie, the expected win percentages will be listed as 52.6% (50/95) and 47.4% (45/95.)

skill, so I've cut the table off at a level that covers all match ups priced within the − 200/+200 range. As mentioned, single round match-up odds are also offered for most tournaments and here's that corresponding cheat sheet.

Heads–Up Expected Win Percentages,
One Round Only

Golfer	Stroke per Round Edge	Expected Win %
A	.25	53%
B		47%
A	.50	56%
B		44%
A	.75	58%
B		42%
A	1.00	61%
B		39%
A	1.25	64%
B		36%
A	1.50	66%
B		34%

Although we don't know the offered matchups yet, let's pretend that like last year, the books offer Jordan Spieth vs. Rory McIlroy, Spieth vs. Justin Thomas and McIlroy vs. Thomas for the full tournament. Last year, all three of those matchups went off at close to even odds, or − 110 a side. If those same matchups were offered this year, here's what my baseline expectancy calculation would look like, before any course history, recent form, or other factors were applied, or changes in PAR calculation since 1/1/19 etc. are considered:

Golfer	PAR	Exp Win % Matrix		
		Thomas	McIlroy	Spieth
Thomas	1.83	x	63%	67%
McIlroy	1.19	37%	x	54%
Spieth	0.96	33%	46%	x

I can't stress enough that those are baseline calculations, before say, course factors are applied, so that my fair value for a Thomas vs. Spieth bet will not be − 203/+203, as a 67% win expectancy would suggest. But, I'm also pretty sure that, if nothing has changed in their level of play during the first three months of 2019, I'm going to have Rory McIlroy and Jordan Spieth ranked materially lower than the oddsmakers will.

That's going to be the starting point for my handicapping of the Masters. Yours may look very different than mine and that's great. As they say, it takes two to make a market. One thing I'm sure we'll agree on, though, is that we can't wait to see how it plays out the second weekend of April.

CHAPTER 8

Beyond the Numbers

When I proposed to my literary agent the idea of a data-centric book on golf one of her first questions was, "Why do you want to write this book?" Although not prepared for the question, I answered it instantly, "Because there are stories to tell in the data that golf fans will love."

I may not be the best person to tell those stories and from a business-opportunity standpoint, maybe the market of book-buying golf fans is quite small, but after a year of immersion in the world of golf data, my conviction in the premise hasn't changed.

Sometimes, as in the case of Tiger Woods unfathomable 89-round positive Strokes Gained streak, today's method of data analysis reveals stories we didn't even know existed at the time. Other times, data might reveal a story and then get out of the way, because the story isn't about numbers.

That's the case in one of my favorite rounds of golf I uncovered in the course of researching 23 years of results on the PGA Tour. In happened at Augusta in 2006 and it's a remarkable story that has nothing to do with Strokes Gained, club head speed, spin rate, or any of the modern devices used to measure success on the golf course. No, this is a story of pride and perseverance, and thanks to the unique nature of the Masters, it could only happen at the Augusta National Golf Club.

As all readers must surely know, the Masters is an invitation-only tournament, and the Augusta National Golf Club actually mails printed invitations to the roughly 90 golfers each year who meet its qualifications for entry. While it's true that no one's invite is a surprise — the criteria for Masters qualification are well-known — it's also true that receiving the letter from Augusta is the highlight of the year for many golfers, especially first-time qualifiers, who have been known in recent years to post the letter on social media.

Word is, there's another letter the Augusta National Golf Club occasionally sends out. Not only will you never see it posted on a golfer's Instagram account, it's a letter no one wants to receive.

Almost to a man, players on the PGA Tour will tell you that the Masters is the best-run tournament of the year. One reason is that the club treats the entire week as an annual gathering of a select group of friends. In that vein, anyone who wins the Masters earns a lifetime invitation to the tournament. Thanks to that arrangement, the history of the Masters is easily shared among golfers — it only takes three degrees of separation to link any golfer to the roots of the tournament and similarly to the legends of the sport. For instance, 19-year old Joaquin Niemann played in his first Masters in 2018 against Tiger Woods. Woods played against Doug Ford, who won the 1957 tournament. Ford competed for a number of years against Horton Smith, the winner of the inaugural Masters, when the tournament was initially known as the Augusta National Invitational.

However, it's been reported that in the early 2000s, after the course had been significantly lengthened and otherwise altered to require more precision and power, the club discreetly started sending letters to some past champions that, rather bluntly, informed them their participation in the tournament was no longer welcome. Some of the older champions were no longer competitive.

The letter (along with a similar one, quietly rescinded, that tried to put an age limit on participation) prompted some hard feelings, became a topic of contention among some old champions and even merited mention during a Jack Nicklaus press conference in 2005. Nicklaus said, half-jokingly (but maybe not) that the 2005 Masters would be his final turn at Augusta because "he didn't want to get 'the letter'." His statement addressed the elephant in the room and also allowed Nicklaus to clearly state retirement was his decision and to clarify that he hadn't gotten "the letter."

We can't know for sure who received those letters in the 2000s, but by 2006 it was pretty clear that 68-year old former champion Charles Coody was at least a candidate for the mailing list. Coody won the 1971 Masters over runners-up Johnny Miller and Nicklaus in an otherwise obscure career on the PGA Tour. Coody won just two other minor tournaments and only had seven other top-ten finishes in the 75 majors he entered over the course of his career. Of course, nearly two dozen of those major tournament participations were in the Masters, well after he'd stopped competing on the Tour.

After a failed effort in the 2005 tournament, Coody had missed the cut in 18 of the last 21 Masters he'd entered, including the last 12 in a row. Worse, his scores were reflective of non-competitiveness as well. The lengthening of the course, which is a demanding walk no matter the length, had clearly taken its toll on Coody. From 2002 through 2005, he shot 82-84, 83-81, 88-79, and 88-83 on the Par 72 course. Whether he'd received the letter or not is anyone's guess, but regardless, Coody had decided that 2006 would be his last Masters.

With an opening round 89 in 2006, his worst ever at Augusta, it clearly looked like the right decision.

Occasionally, professional athletes perform feats that make even those who consume sports on a regular basis ask, "Where did that come from?" How did Tom Brady lead a 4th-quarter comeback in Super Bowl LI after looking so ordinary for three quarters? How did Bob Beamon, or more recently Katie Ledecky, destroy world records at the Olympics typically bested in inches and split seconds by multiples of those measures? It's one of the things that make viewing sports so much fun. Usually we marvel at feats that thrust athletes into winning roles. Sometimes however, amazing accomplishments occur when few notice. That's what happened on Friday, April 7, 2006 in Augusta, Georgia.

Three months short of his 69th birthday, Charles Coody came back to the course that day to play his final round as a professional golfer. He knew that he was, to a certain degree, no longer welcome in the tournament where he had achieved his greatest professional accomplishment. He'd just shot his worst score ever, an embarrassing 89, and he'd only broken 80, and barely at that, once in his last nine efforts at the Masters. And yet, just as not all heroes wear capes, not all magnificent accomplishments end with trophies.

Coming off a round in which he'd only been able to par six of the 18 holes, Coody promptly bogeyed his first hole of Round 2. Then something happened that only a former world-class athlete can explain as Coody began to draw on either muscle memory or some sort of internal fountain of youth. By the time Coody exited Augusta's famed Amen Corner, a dozen holes later, he'd made only *one* more bogey, a mere blemish during that 12-hole stretch when *he also recorded three birdies!* Coody bogeyed 14 but came right back and birdied 15; with three holes left to play in his professional career, Charles Coody was 1-under par at the Masters. Alas, he ended bogey, double bogey, par finishing with a 2-over par, 74.

It's a cliché for athletes to tell the press after an event that, "I'll tell my grandkids about this one," and in truth, as sometimes reflected in the arts, the athlete who does nothing but relive his glory days is a sad study. But Charles Coody got to turn that cliché on its head. He did something in *front* of his grandkids, that they'll remember him by until the day he dies. Fifteen months before his 70th birthday, on the last day of his professional career, when the rest of the field averaged 73.99 strokes on the toughest and most prestigious course on Tour, Charles Coody walked off the 18th green at Augusta having been equal, one last time, to the greatest golfers in the world. With apologies to Bill Murray, *that's* a Cinderella story.

About the Author

Joe Peta is the author of *Trading Bases*, a Top-10 Amazon Best-seller in the disparate categories of baseball, business and sports betting. He was the lead baseball analyst at ESPN Chalk from 2015-2017 and known to readers for his 'perfect bracket' during the 2016 MLB playoffs. He lives in San Francisco with his wife, two daughters and an unmoving double-digit handicap.

Made in the USA
Columbia, SC
06 April 2019